75 Recipes for Making the Most of Your Ingredients

CHARLOTTE DRUCKMAN

KITCHEN REMIX

PHOTOGRAPHS BY AUBRIE PICK

Clarkson Potter/Publishers *New York*

FOR MY BROTHER, JOHN, IN THE
HOPE THAT HE WILL BOIL WATER AND
NEVER STOP MAKING ME LAUGH SO
HARD I SNORT-CHOKE

Published in the United States by Clarkson
Potter/Publishers, an imprint of Random
House, a division of Penguin Random
House LLC, New York.
clarksonpotter.com

CLARKSON POTTER is a trademark and
POTTER with colophon is a registered
trademark of Penguin Random House LLC.

Library of Congress Cataloging-in-
Publication Data
Names: Druckman, Charlotte, author. |
    Pick, Aubrie, photographer.
Title: Kitchen remix : 75 recipes for
    making the most of your ingredients /
    Charlotte Druckman ; photographs by
    Aubrie Pick.
Description: First edition. | New York :
    Clarkson Potter/Publishers, 2019.
Identifiers: LCCN 2018016569 (print)
    | LCCN 2018021632 (ebook) | ISBN
    9780553459692 | ISBN 9780553459685
    | ISBN 9780553459692 (ebook)
Subjects: LCSH: Cooking. | LCGFT:
    Cookbooks.
Classification: LCC TX714 (ebook) |
    LCC TX714 .D73 2019 (print) |
    DDC 641.5—dc23
LC record available at https://lccn.loc.gov
    /2018016569

ISBN 978-0-553-45968-5
Ebook 978-0-553-45969-2

Printed in China

Book and cover design by
Stephanie Huntwork
Cover photographs by Aubrie Pick

Author photograph on page 224 by her
father, James P. Druckman

10 9 8 7 6 5 4 3 2 1

First Edition

CONTENTS

INTRODUCTION

Many of the most adventurous eaters and food-loving citizens I know are intimidated by cooking. They can't wait to visit new restaurants, taste unfamiliar dishes from other cultures and countries, try new sauces or spices they've read about. But they don't feel quite as intrepid at the stove. They have the basics under their belts and are comfortable with a few simple techniques or dishes, if a little bored. They want to incorporate some of what they're experiencing as diners and shoppers into their home kitchens, but they're not sure how. Maybe you're one of them. If so, I wrote *Kitchen Remix* for you.

I've always loved cookbooks. Growing up, I read my mom's, tracking her progress on the page alongside her as she followed a recipe. I cooked from them sometimes, too, and enjoyed it. In 2005, I started writing about food and, three years later, co-founded a somewhat irreverent yet adoring cookbook tournament: Food52's The Piglet, which playfully pits sixteen of the year's best titles against each other, NCAA March Madness–style, recruiting judges like Ina Garten or the late Nora Ephron to weigh in. That's when the cookbooks really began rolling in and filling my shelves. If it bears even the slightest resemblance to a cookbook, I've probably seen it.

My hope is that you'll acquire some essential, adaptable skills and learn how to apply them with imagination. Ultimately, I want to show you that if your main ingredients get along, you can trust them—and yourself—to produce something you'll want to eat.

I've found most of these books fall into one of two broad categories: either they're cheffy, restaurant-style productions containing information meant to impress without necessarily being applicable to the residential kitchen, or they're expressly designed for home cooks and dumbed down, presuming that the average nonprofessional has a limited capacity to learn and an equally stunted palate. If you're curious or passionate about food, you're probably looking at books that are full of things you would love to eat but really don't want to cook, or their opposite: books featuring things easy to make but monotonous to eat.

What kind of cookbook would offer incentive and guidance to these underserved, potentially prolific—or at least mildly active—home cooks? What would satisfy a wide range of cravings and a desire for more sophisticated flavors, and remain in the realm of possibility for anyone untrained or underconfident? I hadn't really thought about it before, despite all that time spent with my nose

in those books, until my brother had what I consider a legitimate food crisis.

John has the best sense of humor of anyone I know. He and I live to prank our other family members and loved ones, but when he asked me how to boil water a few years ago, I knew he wasn't joking. I was aware he didn't cook but assumed he could do enough to fend for himself. How was this possible? We'd grown up with the same parents!

A few weeks after this troubling revelation, I presented my brother with a mini food processor and the gift of a cooking lesson, with me, for Christmas. Getting him in the kitchen wasn't the challenge; figuring out what to do with him once I got him there was. This is a man who spends his weekend afternoons chasing the best dim sum or Greek meze in Queens. He's more likely to order in Peruvian-style rotisserie chicken with spicy-creamy green ají sauce than a plain, griddled breast. And no one has a better working knowledge of the tacos of New York City—all five boroughs.

Between these dining excursions, I knew he tried to stay relatively healthy. I kept that in mind as I thought about the ingredients he gravitates toward. They're easy to find, versatile, and complementary: chicken breast, broccoli, cashew nuts, pineapple, pasta, carrots. I started there and began to contemplate what we could cook with them—and all the possible permutations.

We could do a crisp-skinned cast-iron chicken with olive oil–roasted, brown-'round-the-edges broccoli tossed with salt, lemon, smoked red chili flakes, and toasted cashew nuts. I could teach him how to stir-fry chicken with the brassica, canned pineapple, and nuts, using the leftover juice from the fruit for a marinade. The cashews and broccoli could go in the food processor with garlic, herbs, and some cheese, then olive oil drizzled in to make a pesto for saucing pasta—with or without chicken; redirected, that dish could become a chicken salad,

with or without pasta. The condiment could also have other destinations—spooned on top of roasted carrots or smeared onto a melted-cheese-topped piece of poultry and placed on a roll as a reimagined chicken Parm sandwich.

We got a lot done that afternoon—too much for one person to digest in one sitting, literally and figuratively. I'm not sure which of us was prouder at the end of the day. John no longer needed to be embarrassed about his inability to boil water or to cook. But I had inadvertently discovered a way to get people who are passionate about food into their kitchens to do more than pour a bowl of small-batch granola, toast a few slices of a long-fermented sourdough loaf, brew a cup of microroasted, organic coffee, or, at best, fry up some local farm-fresh eggs and artisanally cured bacon. By focusing on a few compatible, lovable ingredients at a time and offering a bunch of alternative ways to put them together or remix them—I could optimize for manageability and still offer

variation, with a little choose-your-own-adventure thrown in.

So, I wrote this book for John, but really, I wrote it for people who want to make cooking a part of their routine, whether occasionally or multiple times a week. I also wrote it for people who already cook regularly and want to add a few dishes to their rotation, get acquainted with flavors they haven't incorporated much in the past, or learn some novel ways to work with those they frequently turn to.

Are you in the market to acquire some new, nonscary techniques? This book is for you. And if you like or have to cook but are nonplussed by humdrum spaghetti and meatballs, banal baked potatoes, Toll House–ish chocolate-chip cookies, down-the-line mac and cheese, or boxed brownies, this is your cookbook, too.

My hope is that you'll acquire some essential, adaptable skills and learn how to apply them with imagination. Ultimately, I want to show you that if your main ingredients get along, you can trust them—and yourself—to produce something you'll want to eat.

In a way, Kitchen Remix is as much about defining a style of home cooking that feels relevant to our lives today as it is about answering that timeless question: what do I want to eat?

By focusing on a few compatible, lovable ingredients at a time and offering a bunch of alternative ways to put them together—or remix them—I could optimize for manageability and still offer variation, with a little choose-your-own-adventure thrown in.

ABOUT THIS BOOK

Kitchen Remix teaches you how to combine ingredients. It identifies the definitive staples of today's pantry and shows you what you can do with them.

What follows are twenty-five sets of three ingredients, each set with recipes for three very different dishes that include its respective ingredients, and each with a cheat sheet that explains the logic behind its selection and will guide those who wish to adapt recipes or invent new ones. These trios are divided into sections according to their anchoring component: Vegetables, Beans + Grains, Seafood, Poultry + Meat, and Dairy. Most of the featured ingredients are part of the established everyday canon (apples, rice, or tomatoes, for example), with a few newer inductees like radicchio and tahini that I consider modern essentials and, although not necessarily familiar to everyone, are still easy to find at Whole Foods, Trader Joe's, and online. Many are things you probably (and should) already have on call in your kitchen. Some are so commonplace and versatile they've been cast in starring roles twice. Lots make cameos in other recipes—eggs fill batters, olive oil dresses salads, garlic and onions set stews in motion. Additional supporting characters are items I always have around. I've included a list on page 13.

When you've got confidence, making dinner doesn't feel like a chore, even when it is.

If you're a meal planner, you can use this book to organize a few days' worth of cooking by choosing one or two sets of three, shopping for them together, then working through them. Gather a bunch of chicken legs, apples, and shallots (page 150), and you've got three entirely different dinners lined up.

If you're new to the stove, use each triplet to tutor yourself. Start with something as simple as Arborio rice, onions, and Parmesan cheese (page 80), and learn how to prepare risotto, arancini, and quiche. You'll get some basic culinary tasks under your belt and feel comfortable with three ubiquitous ingredients.

If you've already had some practice and want to develop your skills further, you can "cook by the set," too: try the recipes for pork belly (page 184), and you'll get a crash course in how to braise that baby 'til it yields to the slightest prod of a fork, stir-fry it in the blink of an eye, or roast it so its skin crackles like a sheet of brittle. You'll become nimbler, knowing that when you're presented with a piece of meat or fish, you don't have to do the same thing to it every time. With that wisdom comes the ability to cook on the fly. Let's say you stroll through your farmers'

market, spy some freshly foraged mushrooms, and declare them dinner. Bring them home, open the book to page 22, and go for it.

Then there are the ad-libbers. I am hoping you'll find this book a pit stop for brainstorming or scouting a few things to steal and make your own.

Whatever your style in the kitchen, you gotta eat, and you can use this cookbook to get there. If you're looking to mix 'n' match an entire menu or select an item for a specific occasion, there's an appendix where recipes have been organized by purpose—appetizer, main course, snack, and so on (page 214).

George Bernard Shaw wrote that there is "no love sincerer than the love of food." I think that extends beyond eating food to preparing it. Taking pleasure in the act of cooking is a gift, but it's a simple one; it doesn't have to—and shouldn't—be a luxury. The determining factor is confidence. When you've got it, making dinner doesn't feel like a chore, even when it is. That's what I intended *Kitchen Remix* to give you—confidence in your ability to perform a technique, put ingredients together, and end up with something delicious.

With a well-rounded supply of ingredients in your kitchen, you can resourcefully cobble a meal together without having to go to the store all the time. If you're thoughtful enough about which items you stock, a pantry dinner—and breakfast or lunch—can be as impressive as one you planned for days or bought special products for. But having an overcrowded pantry or jam-packed fridge is its own problem—you don't want so much stuff that it goes to waste or takes up precious counter space.

Here, I've outlined my ideal inventory. I believe it strikes a perfect balance. It also happens to be exactly what you'd want on hand if you were going to make most of the recipes in this book—all you'd have to do is procure the necessary fresh produce, if that. I've divided this list according to where the items are stored and broken each section down further, noting the items I deem essentials and which are nice but not necessary.

You'll notice one exception: the selection of spices. Before you ask why that list is so much lengthier and whether you really need so many, I will tell you spices are transforming agents that are crucial to building flavor. Those small seeds and powders are responsible for turning a dish into something Italian, Indian, Mexican, Moroccan,

Japanese, or a wonderful and original combination thereof. You can go anywhere in the world, culinarily, with a pinch or two. They can make even stone soup into the most bewitching of aromatic brews. Plus, they don't take up much room and they have longevity—when whole, they can last for up to four years; when ground, two to three. Some dried herbs peter out after one year, but still! Obviously, the sooner you use them, the more potent they'll be. But if you store them properly, they'll stand you in good stead for a while. Make sure you keep them in airtight containers in a cool dark place. Like vampires, they are zapped of their strength if exposed to direct sunlight.

Always try to seek out the best-quality ingredients you can afford. They really do yield better-tasting results.

PANTRY

DRY GOODS
Necessities
All-purpose flour
Baking chocolate (dark, semi-sweet or bittersweet, and milk)—I use Valrhona baking disks; the Guanaja 70% dark chocolate and Bahibé 46% milk chocolate are my go-tos. You can also work

with bars of chocolate—cut them up into 1 × 1/2-inch rectangles. Ultimately, what matters is getting the best-quality option available to you.

Baking powder
Baking soda
Bread
Bread crumbs or panko crumbs
Brown sugar (light or dark)
Cocoa powder
Cornmeal (fine ground or polenta)
Dried beans
Dried pasta (small shape like orecchiette or longer noodle like spaghetti)
Garlic
Granulated sugar
Oats (old-fashioned rolled or steel-cut)
Potatoes
Rice (long grain like basmati or jasmine, or medium grain like Arborio)

Bonuses
Almond meal/flour
Coconut sugar
Confectioners' sugar
Crackers
Demerara or turbinado sugar
French's Crispy Fried Onions
Instant espresso powder
Sun-dried tomatoes, dry
Toasted nori

SPICES

Allspice, ground
Allspice berries
Aniseeds
Bay leaves, dried
Black mustard seeds
Black peppercorns—Whenever
   a recipe calls for the ground
   stuff, I grind it fresh so I
   get the spice at its most
   concentrated, potent best.
Caraway seeds
Cardamom (green), **ground**
Cardamom pods (green)
Chili pepper flakes
Chili peppers, dried—Consult
   the Scoville scale to find
   the chilies in your desired
   range of heat. Note that a
   pepper's size is inversely
   proportionate to its ability
   to burn.
Cinnamon, ground
Cinnamon sticks
Cloves, whole
Colman's mustard powder
Coriander, ground
Coriander seeds
Cumin, ground
Cumin seeds
Curry powder
Fennel seeds
Ginger, ground
Juniper berries
Nigella seeds
Nutmeg, ground
Nutmeg seeds
Salt—In this book, if a recipe
   doesn't specify type,
   you can assume I mean
   fine table salt or sea salt;
they're interchangeable
in small quantities (up to
1 tablespoon). Other times,
I've called for coarse sea salt,
kosher salt, or flake salt. The
latter is used primarily as
a finishing salt for its light
crunch; Maldon is probably
the best known, while *fleur de
sel*, a strain of flake salt from
Brittany, France, is prized for
its delicate texture and flavor.
You should have a **fine salt**,
kosher salt, and some type of
flake salt in your pantry.
Smoked paprika
Sumac, ground
Thyme, dried
Turmeric, ground
Vanilla beans—Buy your vanilla
   beans in bulk for better value,
   and try to use them within a
   year. If you have any left over,
   make vanilla extract: slice the
   beans open, shove them into
   a small tinted glass bottle,
   and cover with rum, bourbon,
   or vodka. To get the seeds
   out of a vanilla bean, place it
   on a cutting board and use a
   sharp paring knife to split it
   down the middle. Holding the
   tip of the bean, use the dull
   side of the blade to scrape
   the seeds away from the pod,
   swiping vertically, away from
   you, down the entire length,
   from the tip to the base.
White pepper, ground
White sesame seeds
Yellow mustard seeds

CANNED + JARRED GOODS

Necessities

Anchovies, in olive oil
**Canned tomatoes, whole and
   chopped**—I recommend
   San Marzano.
Cannellini beans
Capers, in brine
Chickpeas
Coconut milk
Tuna, in oil

Bonus

Pickles—I like bread-and-
   butter or sweet gherkins.

CONDIMENTS + SPREADS

Necessities

Dijon mustard
Fruit jam
Harissa
Hoisin sauce
Honey
Honey mustard
Hot sauce—You've got to have
   at least one kind, even if the
   mere mention of the word
   spicy makes you start to
   sweat. They come in varying
   degrees of heat, amounts of
   acid, and shades of pepper
   flavor. Some options are
   Tabasco, sriracha, gochujang,
   piri piri, sambal oelek, and
   pepper sauce.
Ketchup
Maple syrup
Mayonnaise
Mirin—This Japanese sweet
   wine, one of the mainstays

of its native country's cuisine, has been adopted into Western cooking. It can be added to other sauces, whisked into vinaigrettes, combined into marinades, and stirred into soups. It's great for mellowing salty flavors or sneaking in a subtle sweetness. You need just a splash or two.

Nut butter

Soy sauce—In Japan and China, what we here think of as "regular" soy sauce is considered "light." For most of us, this is the go-to, and Kikkoman tends to be the brand of choice. There is also dark soy sauce, which I like to keep in my kitchen, too. It's thicker, slightly sweet, and unexpectedly less salty.

Tahini

Tomato paste

Bonuses

Chocolate-hazelnut spread

Date syrup

Mango chutney

Pomegranate molasses

Tomato jam

Worcestershire sauce

OILS

Necessities

Coconut oil—Throughout this cookbook, I call for unrefined coconut oil because I want it to impart its flavor. The refined variant loses much of its coconutty taste and comes close enough to being a neutral oil that you can use it in place of one of those, if it's all you have.

Extra-virgin olive oil

Neutral oil—You'll often see this expression referenced for sautéing or frying. It describes any aroma-less oil that won't interfere with the flavors of your ingredients. Canola, peanut, sunflower, safflower, vegetable, and grapeseed oils all qualify.

Sesame oil

Bonus

Olio nuovo—This translates from the Italian as "new oil," which is exactly what it is—the just-pressed, unfiltered oil from the first-harvested olives among the annual fall crop. Grassy and fruity, sometimes peppery, it's usually recognized by its Kermit-the-Frog green color and intense flavor. As a finishing agent, it brings magic to salad, bread, fresh ricotta, soup, and even gelato. It's my first choice for any olive oil–based baking or dessert-related dish. Don't waste it on sautéing or frying, or anything that shouldn't have a pronounced olive-oil taste.

VINEGARS

Necessities

Balsamic vinegar

Rice vinegar (unseasoned)

Bonuses

Apple cider vinegar

Red wine vinegar

Sherry vinegar

White wine vinegar

Refrigerator

Necessities

Apples

Butter—In this book recipes call for unsalted butter.

Crème fraîche (or sour cream)

Dried fruit

Eggs

Fresh herbs—Parsley, mint, dill, cilantro, chives, oregano, thyme, rosemary, chervil, marjoram, verbena, rose geranium, savory, tarragon . . . they belong in the fridge, except basil, which should be kept on your counter, away from direct sunlight, in a jar with a couple of inches of water. Rinse herbs under cold water, lightly shake them off, run them through a salad spinner, and pat them with a paper towel.

Lemons

Miso—In this cookbook, I use white miso. Also known as *shiro miso*, the fermented soybean paste is considered the "sweet" or "mellow" member of the miso family.

Onions

Parmesan cheese

Plain Greek yogurt (I prefer full fat)

Shallots

Bonuses

Almond milk

Buttermilk

Chinese sausage (*lap cheong*)—You'll find this easily online through specialty Asian purveyors or even Amazon. It's also sold in the markets of Chinatowns across the country.

Labneh

Leeks

Limes

Olives—When you're dealing with especially salty olives, rinse and pat them dry before applying them to your recipe. Kalamata, niçoise, picholine, and Castelvetrano are the varietals suggested in this cookbook.

Oranges

Ricotta, fresh

FREEZER

Necessities

Bacon

Nuts—These will do fine for a few months if you store them in an airtight container at room temperature. But you can keep them in the fridge for six months, or in the freezer for a whole year. This means you can buy them in bulk—a more economical choice—and then use them over a relatively long period of time.

Peas (green)

Vanilla ice cream

Bonuses

Coconut (finely shredded, unsweetened)

Coconut chips (unsweetened)

Stock—Whether you make your own stock or buy good-quality fresh or frozen stock from a specialty market or butcher, it will be better than any of the canned or boxed offerings, although those are fine. Chicken and vegetable stocks are good all-purpose choices.

BLANCHING & SHOCKING

To blanch an ingredient, drop it into boiling water for 1 minute or so to make its skin easier to peel (as with a tomato) or to optimize its color, barely cooking it just until it's bright (as with broccoli rabe). To bring the blanched ingredient's temperature down immediately and stop it from cooking further, plunge it into an ice bath, a process called "shocking."

SALTING PASTA WATER

I like sea salt for this task and stick to a ratio of 2 teaspoons coarse sea salt per quart. Use slightly less fine sea or table salt (1½ teaspoons per quart), or more if you've got an extra-coarse kosher salt (1 tablespoon per quart).

BAKING VESSELS

Metal is the best material for maximizing browning and crispiness, because it gets hotter faster than other materials. If you use a ceramic or glass pie dish, your tart will likely take longer to bake. It will also take longer to cool down, as those surfaces are better at retaining heat.

TOASTING NUTS

There are two ways to toast nuts: in the oven and on the stove top. The first gets you optimal results—more even cooking and intense flavor: preheat the oven to 350°F, spread the nuts on a baking sheet, and pop them in there for anywhere from 5 to 12 minutes, depending on their size and just how dark you want them. The stove top is faster: put them in a dry pan and shake it so they toast evenly, up to 5 minutes, tops, depending on the type. Either way, keep a close watch, as nuts go from toasted to burnt pretty fast. You'll know they're ready when they've released their aroma and begun to brown. If you want more color on them, leave them a little longer. Let them cool completely before using.

TOASTING SPICES

I prefer to toast spices in a preheated 350°F oven until their aroma has intensified and their color slightly deepened. It should take 5 minutes on average, but this will depend on the type of seed. You can also do this on the stove in a heavy-bottomed skillet or even a sauté pan; it's faster. Heat the pan over medium-high heat, and once it's hot, add the seeds and toast them, shaking the pan constantly; on average, this takes 1 to 3 minutes, but again, it will vary according to seed varietal. Remember two things: (1) they're even quicker to burn than nuts, so pay attention, and (2) let your seeds cool before you grind them.

VEGETABLES

POTATO

+

MUSHROOM

+

TALEGGIO

Aromatically, these ingredients are linked to one another like a daisy chain. Potatoes are earthy and, at times, reminiscent of chestnuts. Mushrooms taste of the damp forest soil and have a musky, garlicky funk that can carry hints of hazelnuts. Pudding-thick Taleggio's pungency belies its fruity tang and nuttiness.

	CHARACTER	SUBSTITUTE	TIP	COMPLEMENTS
POTATO	Earthy, starchy, filling	Sweet potato, parsnip, celery root	Roast or boil the small, waxy ones; fry, bake, or mash the big, mealy guys.	Stews, onions, leeks, fish, bacon, roast meat or poultry
MUSHROOM	Loamy, spongy, meaty	Walnuts, chestnuts, eggplant	Roast or grill it whole; chop and sauté it; add it raw, sliced, to salads.	Herbs, garlic, onions, green peas, pasta, cheese, eggs, bacon, beef
TALEGGIO	Creamy, washed rind, fruity	Pont-l'Évêque, fontina, Morbier, Gorgonzola dolce	It's cheese-plate-friendly. When cooking with it, remove the rind before slicing.	Cabbage, leeks, apples, bacon, ham, beef

Sometimes you ask for eggs at a diner and they arrive with an unwelcome occupant: a listless pile of bland, greasy, pale potatoes. Other times, your order comes with a golden mess of french fry—crisp nuggets that melt into a fatty mash after you rip through their crunchy surface. You live for those other times. And you know they'd be even better if someone tossed a couple of complements into that hash—something oozy with a pronounced but promising odor like Taleggio, or made in the shade and pulled up from the earth with a hint of garlic in its spores like wild mushrooms. Eggs—fried sunny-side up with gooey yolks, preferably—are a lovely afterthought to this recipe and best placed on top.

POTATO HASH
serves 4

½ cup plus 3 tablespoons extra-virgin olive oil

3 cups trimmed and thinly sliced mushrooms, such as cremini, shiitake, chanterelle, oyster, or a mix (see 'Shroom to Maneuver, page 27)

½ medium yellow onion, thinly sliced

½ teaspoon salt, plus more to taste

1½ pounds yellow potatoes, such as fingerlings, cut into small cubes

¾ teaspoon smoked paprika, plus more to taste (see Cooking Note)

½ pound Taleggio cheese, rind removed, cut into ½-inch cubes

Heat a large cast-iron skillet on the stove, gradually increasing the heat from low to medium. When the pan is hot, add 3 tablespoons of the olive oil. When the oil is shimmering, add the mushrooms and sauté for about 1 minute, stirring constantly. Add the onion and sauté until soft and just starting to color, stirring occasionally, 12 to 20 minutes. Season with a generous pinch of salt and transfer the mixture to a plate.

In the same skillet over medium heat, add the remaining ½ cup olive oil. When the oil is shimmering, add the potatoes, sprinkle with ½ teaspoon salt, and cook until softened and golden, scraping the bottom of the pan with a wooden spatula to incorporate any sticky bits into the mixture, 45 to 50 minutes (or longer for extra crispness).

Add the mushroom-onion mixture back to the skillet and stir to incorporate. Add the smoked paprika and stir again just to combine. Stir in the Taleggio, continuing to cook the hash just until the cheese starts to melt, then remove the pan from the heat.

Taste and adjust for salt or spice as needed. Serve immediately, while hot and gooey.

COOKING NOTE There are many kinds of smoked paprika. I like Pimentón de la Vera, which is a specific type made in Spain's La Vera region; the chilies are dried over wood fires and take on a distinct, smoky aroma. I prefer the sweet, mild (*dulce*) style for this hash, but if you want some heat with your fire, use a spicier (*picante*) strain. If you don't have Pimentón de la Vera, use Hungarian sweet paprika and blend it with the smoky dried red chili flakes of your choice. Or just go with a hotter Hungarian option. French Piment d'Espelette also works.

I'm going to be officious and insist you treat pizza dough as a kitchen staple; it's a meal-in-waiting. It's also one of many places to rally potatoes with mushrooms and Taleggio. The payoff is a lip-smacking, chewy plank that wields down-to-earth charm drawn from the soil-born taters, the loamy 'shrooms, the fungally funky cheese, and the scent-o'-the-piney rosemary and sage. Once cooked, the potatoes and mushrooms can be stored (separately), tightly covered, in the refrigerator for up to 24 hours, so practice a little time management and give yourself a head start when hosting guests or getting dinner on the table.

FLATBREAD
WITH POTATOES, MUSHROOMS & TALEGGIO

serves 6 as an appetizer or 4 as a main course

- 1 large Yukon Gold potato (about ¾ pound), peeled
- 2 sprigs fresh rosemary
- 3 cloves garlic, peeled and smashed
- 1¼ teaspoons kosher salt, plus more to taste
- 5 tablespoons extra-virgin olive oil, plus more for brushing
- 3 cups cleaned, stemmed, and thinly sliced mushrooms
- ¼ teaspoon freshly ground black pepper, plus more to taste
- All-purpose flour, for rolling
- 2 (12-ounce) balls high-quality store-bought pizza dough
- 4 fresh sage leaves, roughly chopped
- ½ pound Taleggio cheese, rind removed, cut into ½-inch cubes

Preheat the oven to 475°F, placing one rack in the middle and another at the bottom. Line two baking sheets with parchment paper.

In a medium saucepan over medium-high heat, combine the potato, rosemary, 1 clove of garlic, 1 teaspoon of the salt, and enough water to cover everything by 1 inch. Bring to a boil, then reduce the heat to medium-low and simmer, uncovered, until the exterior of the potato has softened but its center remains firm, 6 to 8 minutes. Drain the potato, discarding the rosemary and garlic, and let it dry and cool for 3 minutes. Slice the potato into ¼-inch rounds.

Heat a large cast-iron skillet on the stove, gradually increasing the heat from low to medium. Add 3 tablespoons of the olive oil. When the oil is shimmering, add the remaining 2 cloves of garlic and cook for about 1 minute to infuse the oil, flipping the cloves midway to prevent burning. Add the mushrooms and sauté until they shrink, stirring constantly, about 3 minutes. Season with ¼ teaspoon each salt and pepper. Transfer the mushrooms to a medium bowl and discard the garlic cloves.

On a lightly floured surface, using a lightly floured rolling pin, roll out one ball of dough to a 12-inch rectangular shape about ¼ inch thick and transfer it to a prepared baking sheet. Scatter half of the potato slices on the dough, leaving a ¼-inch perimeter. Liberally brush olive oil over the potatoes and dough. Sprinkle on half the sage, followed by half the mushrooms. Scatter half the cheese on top. Drizzle with 1 tablespoon olive oil and season with salt and pepper. Repeat with the second ball of dough and the remaining ingredients on the other baking sheet.

Bake the flatbreads until the crusts have just turned golden, their edges begin to brown, and the cheese is bubbling, 12 to 15 minutes, rotating the sheets and switching their racks halfway through baking.

Transfer the flatbreads to a cutting board. Let cool about 5 minutes, then cut into squares with a sharp knife and serve right away.

Although titled *My Pizza*, no-knead-dough god Jim Lahey's cookbook is one of the best resources for salad recipes. He has two I've made so many times I've lost count: one is a bowlful of raw shiitakes and celery tossed with lemon juice, olive oil, and Parmesan; the other, those same uncooked mushrooms, radicchio, and Taleggio dressed with olive oil and balsamic vinegar. I pretended they were written as a single recipe and that Jim meant for it to showcase the wee-est spuds. This "assumption" leads to a more substantial, complex dish with a contrast of raw and cooked ingredients. Serve it slightly warm or at room temperature and, if your celery comes with its leaves intact, throw them in with the parsley.

NEW POTATO SALAD

serves 4 to 6

1½ pounds baby potatoes, scrubbed and halved

1 teaspoon salt, plus more to taste

5 anchovies packed in olive oil, drained and finely chopped

Juice of 1 lemon

Freshly ground black pepper to taste

¼ cup plus 1½ tablespoons extra-virgin olive oil

½ cup roughly chopped fresh flat-leaf parsley

4 medium stalks celery, thinly sliced (about 1½ cups)

20 medium shiitake mushrooms, stemmed and thinly sliced (about 3 cups), (see 'Shroom to Maneuver)

¼ pound Taleggio cheese, torn into small pieces

In a medium saucepan set over medium-high heat, cover the potatoes with an inch of cold water and 1 teaspoon salt. Bring to a boil, then reduce the heat to medium-low and simmer, uncovered, until the potatoes are fork-tender, 5 to 10 minutes.

Meanwhile, place the anchovies in a large bowl.

Drain the potatoes, transfer them to the bowl with the anchovies, add half of the lemon juice, a generous pinch of salt, and a few grinds of pepper, and toss to coat. Let the hot potatoes sit for 7 minutes to absorb the lemon juice. Add ¼ cup of the olive oil and the parsley, and stir to coat. Set aside to marinate and cool.

Meanwhile, in a medium bowl, add the celery, mushrooms, and the remaining lemon juice, and toss to combine. Drizzle with the remaining 1½ tablespoons olive oil and season with salt and pepper.

Add the dressed celery and mushrooms to the bowl with the potatoes and gently stir to combine. Dot with the Taleggio and toss again. Taste and adjust the seasoning as needed.

'SHROOM TO MANEUVER

When a recipe calls for mixed mushrooms, what kind should you use? Any and all kinds! The shiitake is my go-to. Then there are the slightly fancier black trumpet and hen of the woods, to which I'm partial, and the hoity-toity chanterelles and morels I hate myself for loving, but man, are they intensely good. The basic button is as trusty as they come. Don't forget the gilled oyster! The big-top portobello is nice and meaty—I prefer its mini-me, the cremini, but they're interchangeable. And you can always go with a medley, mixing those you like, depending on what's available and in season at your local market.

No matter the type, mushrooms attract a noticeable amount of dirt—they thrive in damp soil—but it's easy to remove. For sturdier mushrooms, or those with a heavier coating of grit, a soft brush is best. Otherwise, you can just rub a damp paper towel over the surface to wipe them clean. Another option would be to quickly place them in a bowlful of water and use your hands to gently toss them through it; you'll see the dirt sink to the bottom of the bowl. Then you can place them on a clean towel and pat them dry. If you're eating them raw, the water bath isn't ideal for optimal texture. And if you're cooking them, be sure to do the washing right before you plan to use them and dry them well!

CAULIFLOWER
+
BACON
+
CAPERS

Cauliflower can carry a meal, but it's kind of low energy. It needs perking up—and that starts with salt. Bacon is an effective way to add that essential flavoring along with fat and protein. The pickled flower buds we call capers come in with a corresponding sour salinity.

	CHARACTER	SUBSTITUTE	TIP	COMPLEMENTS
CAULIFLOWER	Cruciferous, firm, sweet	Broccoli, romanesco, cabbage, steak, extra-firm tofu	Grate it to imitate couscous or replace flour in pizza or savory tart crusts.	Sweet bell peppers, pasta, hazelnuts, almonds, cheese, sausage, shrimp, scallops
BACON	Salty, smoky, fatty	Smoked mozzarella, prosciutto, pancetta, ham, chorizo, smoked turkey	Crisp slices in a 400°F oven; render fat on the stove over medium-low heat.	Onions, mushrooms, tomatoes, corn, cabbage, greens, prunes, potatoes, pasta, beans, cheese, eggs, clams, crab
CAPERS	Briny, acidic, firm	Green olives, caper berries, dill pickles, brined green peppercorns, fresh herbs seasoned with lemon juice	If they're packed in brine, rinsing is optional; in salt, rinse, soak, and rinse again.	Sweet-and-sour preparations, balsamic vinegar, brown butter, raisins, potato salad, seafood, steak (cooked or raw)

When Meera Sodha's *Fresh India* arrived from the UK, the first page I turned to was a photo of cauliflower korma scattered with charred raisins and almonds. Originally, korma referred to an Indian curry perfected in the kitchens of Moghul emperors. This yogurt-braised meat dish was made extra thick with ground nuts, and it radiated warmth, thanks to aromatics like cinnamon, cardamom, and ginger. Today, korma can describe any mild curry. I began adapting Sodha's recipe, as one does, replacing her combination of milk and yogurt with kefir, undermining her vegetarian agenda with bacon, and recruiting Chinese five-spice powder to fill in for garam masala. The blackened raisins remain; they're paired with capers, recalling the sweet-and-sour preparations of Sicily. It's no korma, but I'm not complaining.

SAUCED ROASTED CAULIFLOWER

serves 4 to 6

- 2 large heads of cauliflower (about 3½ pounds total), cut into florets
- 6 tablespoons extra-virgin olive oil
- 1½ teaspoons salt
- 1 teaspoon freshly ground black pepper
- 5 ounces bacon, sliced crosswise into ¾-inch-wide strips
- 3 tablespoons drained brined capers
- 3 tablespoons black or golden raisins
- 6 medium to large shallots, peeled, thinly sliced
- 2 teaspoons Chinese five-spice powder
- 2 tablespoons honey
- 2 cups kefir

Preheat the oven to 425°F.

In a large bowl, toss the cauliflower with the olive oil and season with 1 teaspoon of the salt and ½ teaspoon of the pepper. Spread out the florets on two baking sheets. Roast, tossing occasionally, until the cauliflower is tender and golden with some browning around the edges, about 45 minutes.

Meanwhile, heat a large cast-iron skillet on the stove, gradually increasing the heat from low to medium. Add the bacon and cook, stirring a few times, until it's crisp and the fat has been rendered, about 10 minutes. Using a slotted spoon, transfer the bacon to a paper-towel-lined plate to cool. Drain the skillet, reserving 3 tablespoons of the rendered fat.

Wipe out the skillet and return it to medium heat. When the pan is hot, add the capers and raisins and fry them, shaking the pan constantly, until the capers have begun to turn brown and the raisins to char, 3 to 4 minutes. Transfer them to a small bowl, keeping the skillet over medium heat.

Add the reserved bacon fat to the skillet. When the fat is shimmering, add the shallots and sauté, stirring frequently, until caramelized, 12 to 15 minutes. Add the remaining ½ teaspoon black pepper, the Chinese five-spice powder, honey, and the remaining ½ teaspoon salt, and sauté for 3 minutes more to let the flavors deepen.

Add the kefir and reduce the heat to medium-low. Cook until the sauce reduces by at least three-fourths and thickens up, stirring occasionally and scraping the base and sides of the pan, about 30 minutes.

Add the roasted cauliflower to the sauce, stirring to coat. Transfer the sauced cauliflower to a serving bowl and stir in the bacon to combine. Sprinkle the raisins and capers over the top and serve.

True or false: People will eat anything if you give it a bubbling crust of bread crumbs and cheese. I'm going with true. Generations of cooks have relied on this scheme to get their kids—and spouses—to eat their veggies. For me, cauliflower doesn't need to be incentivized, but it happens to do especially well in casseroles because it holds its structure beneath all their weighty lures. This casserole has its fair share of them: salty pork fat; a creamy, flour-thickened béchamel sauce; and the requisite blanketing of cheese and bread crumbs. Because this vegetable takes to assertive flavors so well, you can put a few zingers in there, like orange zest, thyme, and—the best surprise of all—those capers.

CAULIFLOWER GRATIN

serves 4

1 medium head cauliflower (about 1½ pounds), cut into 1-inch florets

4½ tablespoons unsalted butter, plus more for greasing

3 tablespoons all-purpose flour

1½ cups whole milk

½ teaspoon salt, plus more to taste

¼ teaspoon freshly ground black pepper

½ teaspoon ground allspice

8 ounces bacon, sliced crosswise into ½-inch-wide strips

3½ tablespoons extra-virgin olive oil

¼ cup bread crumbs

1 tablespoon fresh thyme leaves

½ teaspoon orange zest

¼ pound halloumi cheese, coarsely grated

2 tablespoons Dijon mustard

¼ cup drained brined capers

Prepare an ice bath in a large bowl. Bring 3 quarts water to a boil in a large pot over high heat. Salt the water as you would for pasta. Add the cauliflower and cook for 2 minutes, then drain it and place it in the ice bath. Once the cauliflower has cooled, drain it again and transfer to a large bowl.

Make the béchamel sauce. Melt 3 tablespoons of the butter in a small heavy-bottomed saucepan over medium heat. Reduce the heat to low, add the flour, and cook, stirring continuously, until it begins to take on some color, 2 to 3 minutes. Remove the pan from the heat and when the bubbles have subsided, whisk in the milk until combined. Return to medium heat and continue whisking, scraping up the sauce from the bottom of the pan. As it begins to thicken, after about 3 minutes, whisk in ½ teaspoon salt, the pepper, and allspice. Reduce the heat to medium-low and continue cooking, stirring occasionally, until thickened, 3 to 4 minutes. Transfer the sauce to a small bowl, placing plastic wrap on its surface.

Preheat the oven to 350°F. Grease an 8 × 8-inch casserole dish.

Heat a large cast-iron skillet on the stove, gradually increasing the heat from low to medium. Add the bacon and cook, stirring a few times, until it's crisp and the fat has been rendered, about 10 minutes. Using a slotted spoon, transfer the bacon to a paper-towel-lined plate to cool. Drain the skillet, rinse, and dry.

Return the skillet to medium heat. Add the remaining 1½ tablespoons butter and 1½ tablespoons of the olive oil. When the butter is melted, add the bread crumbs and cook until brown and crispy, stirring frequently, 3 to 4 minutes. Immediately transfer the bread crumbs to a medium bowl. Toss through the thyme, orange zest, and halloumi.

Season the cauliflower with a pinch of salt. Pour the béchamel over it and stir to coat. Stir in the Dijon mustard, bacon, and capers. Transfer the cauliflower mixture to the prepared baking dish. Sprinkle with the bread crumb–halloumi topping. Drizzle up to 2 tablespoons olive oil over the top.

Bake until the top is golden brown and the gratin is bubbling, 30 to 35 minutes. Serve hot.

Whether because of the literary acclaim of its chef Gabrielle Hamilton or her resolve to do whatever the hell she pleases and damn the consequences, Prune has become one of New York City's high-profile restaurants. Its most iconic dish, debatably, is the fried sweetbreads doused in a caper-dotted brown-butter sauce, garnished with a curling slice of bacon. Once tasted, it's the kind of thing you hunger for at home. Preparing pancreatic matter is a major deterrent, but if you try it with cauliflower and a less complicated *grenobloise* sauce comprised of the same ingredients—plus a brisk burst of lemon—you get similar results without breaking a sweat.

CAULIFLOWER À LA PRUNE
(THE RESTAURANT)

serves 2 as a main course or 4 as a side

- 4 slices thinly cut bacon (about ¹⁄₁₆ inch thick)
- ¼ cup all-purpose flour
- 2 large eggs, beaten
- 1½ cups panko crumbs, finely ground
- ¾ teaspoon salt, plus more to taste
- ¾ teaspoon freshly ground black pepper, plus more to taste
- 1 medium head cauliflower (about 1½ pounds), cut into 1- to 1½-inch florets
- Peanut oil, for frying
- 6 tablespoons (¾ stick) unsalted butter
- 2 tablespoons drained brined capers
- Juice of 1 lemon (about 3 tablespoons)
- 2 tablespoons roughly chopped fresh flat-leaf parsley

Place the bacon in a large cast-iron skillet and set it over medium-low heat. When the bacon starts to sizzle, about 7 minutes, increase the heat to medium. Using tongs, flip it over repeatedly as it cooks until it's crispy and the fat has been rendered, 8 to 10 minutes more. Transfer the finished strips to a paper-towel-lined plate to drain. Drain the skillet, rinse, and dry.

Set up a dredging station with three small bowls in a row, the first filled with the flour, the second with the eggs, and the third with the ground panko seasoned with ¾ teaspoon salt and ¾ teaspoon pepper. Dredge each piece of cauliflower through the flour, then dunk it completely into the egg wash, draining any excess, and drop it in the panko mixture, gently rolling it to coat evenly. Transfer to a wire rack.

Meanwhile, heat 3 inches of peanut oil in a large heavy-bottomed pot over medium-high heat until a deep-fry thermometer registers 350°F. Working in batches, fry the cauliflower, turning, until golden brown on all sides, about 3 minutes. Remove with a slotted spoon and drain on paper towels. Immediately sprinkle with a pinch of salt. Transfer to a serving platter.

Melt the butter in a small saucepan over medium-low heat. Continue to cook, swirling constantly, until it turns a deep brown and smells nutty, about 7 minutes. Remove the pan from the heat and add the capers, lemon juice, and parsley, swirling the pan to combine.

Spoon the sauce over the cauliflower. Top with the bacon. Season liberally with pepper. Serve immediately.

BROCCOLI

+

LEEK

+

CHICKEN STOCK

Homemade or store-bought, chicken stock gives body to soups, sauces, stews, braises, and even porridges. It is also a source of protein and adds savory depth to vegetables that have a low-key sweetness, like broccoli with its sharp, cabbage-like tendencies, and grassy leeks, the mellow sibling of the allium family.

	CHARACTER	SUBSTITUTE	TIP	COMPLEMENTS
BROCCOLI	Cruciferous, green, firm	Cauliflower, romanesco, broccolini, broccoli rabe, Brussels sprouts, asparagus	Don't throw out your stalks; they're edible and nutritious. Peel, then thinly slice them.	Beef, chicken, sausage, almonds, cheese, pasta
LEEK	Oniony, grassy, fibrous	Chives, onions, scallions, shallots, ramps	Boil trimmed leeks in salted water until soft, let cool, and drizzle with a mustardy vinaigrette.	Mushrooms, potatoes, winter squash, grapes, Brie, shellfish, meaty white-fleshed fish, chicken, pork chop, bacon, lamb
CHICKEN STOCK	Enriching, savory, moistening	Vegetable stock, beef stock, bouillon cubes, dashi, heavy cream, white wine	Save leftover chicken carcasses and vegetable scraps to make stock. Simmer them with fresh herbs.	Rice, beans, poultry

No one has any business reinventing broccoli soup. But recently, a quick extra step in the preparation caught on: sear the vegetable on only one side, to draw out some of its natural sweetness without losing its green flavor (or color) entirely. It's a small, thoughtful adjustment you can apply to any broccoli soup. I just happen to like my version best, because it includes the restrained oniony-ness of leeks and slightly sugared, earthy bent of parsnips, balanced by the warm, bitter notes of caraway and cumin seeds. Chicken stock rounds out those flavors instead of masking them the way cream would. Make each bowl a little more special with some fresh ricotta and a drizzle of olive oil, or a dollop of crème fraîche.

BROCCOLI LEEK SOUP

serves 4 to 6

- 6 tablespoons extra-virgin olive oil
- 1 bunch broccoli (about 2 pounds), separated into small florets, stalks peeled and diced
- 3 teaspoons salt, plus more to taste
- 4 tablespoons (½ stick) unsalted butter
- 4 leeks, sliced into quarter moons and rinsed (see page 38)
- 4 cloves garlic, thinly sliced
- 2 teaspoons caraway seeds
- 1 teaspoon cumin seeds
- 1 teaspoon freshly ground black pepper, plus more to taste
- 2 parsnips, diced
- 1 quart chicken stock

In a large pot, heat 2 tablespoons of the olive oil over high heat. When the oil is shimmering, add about a third of the broccoli, just enough to cover the bottom of the pan without overcrowding. Cook without moving it until it is dark brown on one side, 4 to 5 minutes. Transfer to a large bowl and repeat in two more batches with the remaining broccoli and oil. Season the finished broccoli with 1 teaspoon of the salt.

Add the butter, leeks, garlic, caraway, cumin, 1 teaspoon of the salt, and the pepper to the pot and cook over medium-low heat until the leeks are wilted and the garlic is translucent, 12 to 15 minutes. Increase the heat to medium and add the parsnips and ½ to 1 teaspoon of the salt. Cook until the parsnips take on some color, about 5 minutes.

Add the chicken stock. Bring the mixture to a simmer and cover. Continue to simmer, adjusting the heat as needed, until the parsnips are just tender, about 10 minutes. Return the broccoli to the pot, cover it again, and continue to simmer, adjusting the heat as needed, until it is tender, 20 to 30 minutes.

Transfer the soup to a blender and puree until your desired consistency is reached. Taste and adjust the seasoning with more salt and pepper as needed.

Ladle into bowls and serve hot. You can make the soup in advance and store it in a sealed container in the fridge for up to 5 days or in the freezer for a couple of months.

COOKING NOTE Making soup is a great way to use up any produce you've got lying around. Don't get stuck on specific ingredients or fixed amounts of them. If you already have carrots, no need to buy parsnips. If your leeks are huge and the broccoli eensy, your batch won't be anything short of good.

I joke that my style of cooking is "weird but good." This recipe is a perfect example. Charring leeks before you incorporate them into a recipe intensifies their sweetness and gives you some of that near-burnt smokiness (just remember to leave their roots attached while you darken them to keep the vegetable intact). I learned to cream them, like spinach, but my version has less dairy; I added chicken stock to compensate. The obscenely rich mixture cooks down to something slightly more substantial than a sauce. I like to top it with browned, roasted broccoli and then, before digging in, to stir the latter into the former . . . because I'm weird, but also because it's good!

CREAMED LEEKS
WITH ROASTED BROCCOLI

serves 2 as a main course or 4 as a side

- 4 leeks, dark green parts removed
- 5 tablespoons plus 2 teaspoons extra-virgin olive oil
- 1 bunch broccoli (about 2 pounds), separated into small florets, stalks peeled and thinly sliced into rounds
- 6 scallions, light green and white parts, thinly sliced
- 2 cloves garlic, finely chopped
- 2 cups heavy cream
- ⅔ cup chicken stock
- 1 tablespoon finely chopped fresh mint
- ½ teaspoon salt
- ½ teaspoon freshly ground black pepper
- ¼ lemon
- 1 teaspoon kosher salt, plus more to taste
- Dried red chili flakes (preferably smoked) to taste

Cut the leeks in half lengthwise, keeping the root intact. Rinse (see page 38) and pat dry.

Heat a cast-iron skillet on the stove, gradually increasing the heat from low to high. Drizzle the leeks with 1 tablespoon of the oil to coat evenly. When the pan is hot, add 4 of the leek halves and cook, flipping occasionally, until slightly charred, about 8 minutes. Transfer to a plate to cool. Repeat with the remaining leek halves.

In a medium bowl, toss the broccoli with 2 tablespoons plus 2 teaspoons olive oil to coat. Set aside.

Cut the cooled leeks into 1-inch pieces, discarding the roots. Heat the remaining 2 tablespoons oil in a medium saucepan over medium heat. When the oil is shimmering, add the scallions and garlic, and cook until tender, stirring once or twice, 3 to 5 minutes. Stir in the cream, chicken stock, and leeks until combined. Continue to cook until the leeks are tender and the cooking liquid has reduced by at least three-fourths

and thickened substantially; the consistency will be similar to that of creamed spinach. Adjust the heat as needed to maintain an even boil, and use a wooden spoon or spatula to stir or scrape along the bottom and sides of the pan occasionally to prevent sticking or burning, 60 to 70 minutes. The mixture will thicken up rather quickly in the last few minutes and start to move as a single mass. Remove the pan from the heat. Stir in the mint, salt, and pepper.

Meanwhile, preheat the oven to 450°F. Spread the broccoli onto a baking sheet and roast for 40 minutes until brown. Remove from the oven and immediately squeeze the lemon on top and sprinkle with 1 teaspoon kosher salt and a pinch or two of chili flakes. Toss to combine. Taste and adjust the seasoning as needed.

To serve, divide the leeks among plates and top each with some of the broccoli.

I had no grievance against vegetables as a kid, with one exception: the string bean. So I was surprised when a recipe for *fasolakia ladera*, a Greek dish of green beans braised in oil, piqued my curiosity. Sliced very thin and cooked until wilted like spaghetti, they looked like they might win me over, and they did—or the method did, if not the beans themselves. I practiced the same technique on broccoli, which, let's admit, is the superior vegetable. It's also easier to prep and yields a chunkier product that's closer to porridge. Spoon it over pasta or soft polenta (page 122), or heap it onto a hunk of bread with shaved aged Parmesan or a gob of ricotta or labneh (see page 192).

BROCCOLI BRAISED IN OLIVE OIL

serves 6 to 8

Extra-virgin olive oil

3 leeks, light green and white parts, finely sliced and rinsed (see below)

1 medium carrot, peeled and finely chopped

1 bunch broccoli (about 2 pounds)

2 teaspoons salt, plus more to taste

¾ cup white wine

1½ cups chopped canned tomatoes

2 cups chicken stock

1 teaspoon sugar

1 dried bay leaf

Freshly ground black pepper to taste

Heat ½ inch of oil in a large pot over medium-high heat. When the oil is shimmering, add the leeks and carrot, and cook until the leeks are soft and glistening, about 10 minutes. Add the broccoli and salt, and cover. Cook until the broccoli is bright green and begins to soften but retains some of its bite, 8 to 10 minutes. Add the wine and continue to cook, covered, until the alcohol has evaporated, 8 to 10 minutes. Add the tomatoes, bring to a boil, and cook for 8 minutes.

Add the stock, sugar, and bay leaf, and reduce the heat to medium. Simmer, uncovered, until the broccoli is tender and has lost most of its color, and most of the liquid has evaporated, 1¾ to 2 hours. Stir occasionally to prevent any sticking, and adjust the heat as needed to maintain the simmer.

Discard the bay leaf. Season with pepper and additional salt as needed. Use a slotted spoon to transfer the broccoli to a serving dish. You can make this ahead and refrigerate it, in a sealed container, for up to a week. Serve hot or at room temperature.

HOW TO CLEAN LEEKS

Leeks are notoriously gritty, but cleaning them isn't as hard as you'd think. You don't even need to soak them. There's an easier way! Trim off the dark-green, fibrous stalk and split the leek lengthwise, keeping the root end intact. Rinse it under cold running water, flipping its layers under the faucet like the pages of a book; any trapped debris will be flushed right out. Alternatively, if your recipe requires you to chop your leeks before cooking them, you can place the pieces in a colander and wash them in there.

ZUCCHINI
+
PISTACHIOS
+
MINT

From ratatouille to tempura, there's so much to be done with pleasantly neutral, omnipresent zucchini. Refreshing and brightening mint bounces off the courgette like reflected light, while grounding, softly crunchy pistachios have the fat and protein to offset the vegetal auras of both the herb and the summer squash.

	CHARACTER	SUBSTITUTE	TIP	COMPLEMENTS
ZUCCHINI	Mild, versatile, high water content	Eggplant, pattypan squash, yellow crookneck squash, broccoli; carrots, apples (for baking)	When dealing with shredded or grated zucchini, drain it and squeeze out all excess water.	Sweet bell peppers, pasta, feta, shrimp, lamb
PISTACHIOS	Earthy, sweet, nubby	Almonds, cashews, hazelnuts, macadamia nuts, pine nuts, pumpkin seeds, sunflower seeds	Make pistachio butter—toast the nuts and blend them in a food processor with salt.	Apricots, cherries, peaches, raspberries, strawberries, mushrooms, beets, sweet potatoes, potatoes, quinoa, farro, feta, lamb
MINT	Cooling, cleansing, bright	Basil, lemon verbena, oregano, rosemary, tarragon; 1 tablespoon chopped mint = 1 teaspoon dried	Refrigerate fresh mint sprigs in a glass with an inch of water, covered and sealed.	Fruit, coconut, ginger, green peas, feta, grain salads, shellfish, lamb, chocolate

It was love at first sight: a photo in a cookbook of wilted zucchini that had been slowly cooked so it could no longer hold its shape but hadn't succumbed to utter mush just yet. Not one to be taken in by dainty, futzed-with platefuls, I was instantly smitten with its blatantly delicious appearance. Here, I've done it my way: stinking it up, seductively, with anise and mint, and making it into something of a porridge with some creamy labneh and a dusting of pistachios to stir through the vegetable. Know what else this zucchini can do? Sauce pasta, bind a rice salad, cover a slice of toast, or make you reconsider the whole creamed-spinach thing by standing in as a side dish.

SLOW-COOKED ZUCCHINI
WITH GROUND PISTACHIOS

serves 4

¼ cup extra-virgin olive oil, plus more for drizzling

2 tablespoons (¼ stick) unsalted butter

5 medium zucchini, trimmed and thinly sliced into ⅛-inch-thick rounds

2 medium cloves garlic, peeled and crushed

1¾ teaspoons salt, plus more to taste

2½ tablespoons roughly chopped fresh mint

1 teaspoon aniseeds

1½ teaspoons freshly ground black pepper

Labneh or full-fat Greek yogurt, for serving

½ cup ground shelled salted roasted pistachios

Heat the olive oil and butter together in a large heavy-bottomed pan or Dutch oven over medium heat. When the butter has melted, add the zucchini and stir to coat. Add the garlic and ¼ teaspoon of the salt. Reduce the heat to medium-low, cover, and continue to cook, stirring occasionally, until the zucchini starts to fall apart and become almost jam-like, about 1 hour.

Remove the pan from the heat and add the mint, aniseeds, pepper, and the remaining 1½ teaspoons salt. Stir to incorporate the seasonings and any residual cooking liquid; the mixture will resemble green porridge.

Taste and adjust the salt as needed. To serve, evenly divide the zucchini among 4 bowls, topping each with a dollop of labneh, a generous drizzling of extra-virgin olive oil, and 2 tablespoons ground pistachios.

I was always confused by zucchini's presence on a crudités platter. I assumed the presiding host couldn't tell his courgette from his cucumber—who would want to eat the stuff raw? Then I had a salad in Florence: cabbage, avocado, and the summer squash, yes, *raw*, with pine nuts. I've been making zucchini salads ever since, and this is one of the greats. The feta soaks in olive oil infused with fresh mint and, to slap your taste buds, a bit of orange zest and chili flakes. Prepare the cheese in advance; the longer it sits, the more flavor it—and the oil—picks up. The feta provides salt, while its marinade becomes a dressing, which is quite convenient and makes the raw zucchini sing.

MINTY-FRESH ZUCCHINI SALAD
WITH MARINATED FETA

serves 4

¼ pound block of feta cheese, cut into squares

Ample bunch of fresh mint leaves, plus more torn leaves for garnish

Freshly ground black pepper to taste

2 or 3 (1-inch) strips orange peel, plus grated zest for garnish

Dried red chili flakes to taste (optional)

Extra-virgin olive oil

2 medium zucchini, cut into 1½ × ½-inch batons (about 5½ cups)

1 teaspoon flake salt

½ cup shelled salted roasted pistachios

¼ cup dried currants

Between 1 day and 2 weeks before serving, place the feta in a 16-ounce jar. Add a generous amount of fresh mint leaves, packing them in as tightly as you can without breaking up the cheese. Add black pepper, the orange peel, and, if you want, a pinch or two of chili flakes. Fill the jar with enough extra-virgin olive oil to just cover the contents, being sure the cheese is completely submerged. Close the jar and turn it over a few times. If you plan to use the cheese the next day, you can keep the jar out at room temperature. Otherwise, place it in the refrigerator.

Place the zucchini in a large serving bowl and season with the salt. Toss to coat. Add the pistachios and the currants and toss to combine.

Remove the cheese from the marinade, letting any excess olive oil drain back into the jar, crumble it into the salad, and toss to combine. The cheese will start to coat the zucchini as you mix everything.

Drizzle 1 tablespoon of the marinating oil over the salad and toss to coat. Garnish the salad with torn fresh mint leaves, additional black pepper, and some grated orange zest.

> **COOKING NOTE** You can reserve the remaining marinade in the fridge for up to 2 weeks and apply it to other salads, on its own or as part of a vinaigrette. Use it for roasting vegetables and poaching fish. Or dip bread into it. Same goes for the feta: toss it into a Greek or grilled-chicken salad. Add it to garlicky shrimp or a grilled sausage dish. Make a simple spaghetti with it—and that oil—too.

My first meeting with pastry chef Melissa Weller began when I showed up at her doorstep and made myself at home in her kitchen. It wasn't trespassing; it was journalism—the kind where you scribble some notes and eat lots of baked goods. That afternoon, the one thing I was unable to try was her zucchini bread. She'd filled it with summer savory, oregano, thyme, olive oil, and walnuts. I had become allergic to those nuts the summer I turned seventeen. But I loved the idea of putting olive oil and fresh herbs in there, and I wanted a loaf I could eat. If you're not allergic, I won't be offended if you try it her way.

ZUCCHINI BREAD

makes two 8 × 4-inch loaves

2 small zucchini

2 cups all-purpose flour, plus more for the pans

1 teaspoon baking powder

½ teaspoon baking soda

1 teaspoon fine sea salt

½ teaspoon freshly ground black pepper

1⅓ cups sugar

3 large eggs

1 cup extra-virgin olive oil, plus more for greasing

¾ cup shelled salted roasted pistachios, roughly chopped

2 tablespoons roughly chopped fresh mint

Preheat the oven to 350°F. Grease and flour two 8 × 4-inch loaf pans. If desired, line with parchment paper.

Grate the zucchini using the large holes of a box grater onto a kitchen towel (you should have about 2½ cups), then squeeze out the excess liquid.

In a medium bowl, sift together the flour, baking powder, baking soda, salt, and pepper. In a large bowl, whisk together the sugar and eggs. Gradually whisk in the olive oil, pouring it in a steady stream. Add the dry ingredients to the wet ingredients, gently stirring to combine. Then add the zucchini, pistachios, and mint, gently stirring to incorporate.

Divide the mixture between the prepared pans. Bake, rotating halfway through, until the tops are light golden and a tester inserted into the centers comes out clean, 45 to 50 minutes.

Let the loaves cool for 10 minutes and then remove them from the pans. Wrapped in aluminum foil or plastic wrap, or sealed in a plastic bag, the zucchini bread can be stored at room temperature for up to 2 days, or refrigerated for a week.

CARROT
+
CASHEWS
+
COCONUT

In this fluid grouping, each ingredient is a dexterous culinary cross-dresser. Carrots can go in cinnamon-spiced Morning Glory muffins or cumin-scented, power-lunch salads with avocado; cashews, in caramel-centered chocolate turtles or Cantonese American chicken stir-fries; and coconut, in graham cracker–crusted "magic bars" or chili-hot Thai massaman curry. It's a switch-hitting ménage à trois.

	CHARACTER	SUBSTITUTE	TIP	COMPLEMENTS
CARROT	Sweet, crisp, root	Winter squash, sweet potato, parsnip, beet, celery, cucumber, zucchini	Peeling is optional so long as you wash and scrub them with a vegetable brush.	Apples, oranges, pineapple, ginger, honey, maple, sesame, chickpeas, green peas, nuts, feta, goat cheese, chicken
CASHEWS	Sweet, meaty, smooth	Almonds, chestnuts, hazelnuts, macadamia nuts, pistachios, peanuts	Toasted raw and roasted nuts are interchangeable. Try swapping in store-bought honey-roasted or spice-dusted cashews.	Caramel, chocolate, butterscotch, bananas, sweet bell peppers, chicken, duck, shrimp
COCONUT	Sweet, nutty, soothing	Butter, neutral oil, avocado (for oil); nut butters (for butter); oats, nuts (for flakes); nut milks (for milk)	For optimal flavor, toast your coconut flakes as you would nuts.	Bananas, lime, pineapple, bell peppers, eggplant, ginger, lemongrass, chilies, dates, rice, seafood, chicken, lamb, chocolate

This salad is sorta like Thai *som tam*. I can never stop eating that spicy, sour, peanut-topped green papaya salad; it's so refreshing, and its gradually building heat has a confoundingly addictive quality. I am predisposed to make it because the dressing is formed from a paste ground in a mortar and pestle, and I'll take any opportunity to pummel my ingredients. You'll see how rewarding that can be when you make this carrot salad. It has a similar balance of flavors, but it's a bit sweeter thanks to the finely shredded coconut, which gives the carrots an agreeable, scratchy texture. And I use cashews in place of peanuts because those crescent-shaped nuts bring out the best in the rest. Like I said, *sorta*.

THAI-ISH CARROT SALAD

serves 4

- 4 medium cloves garlic, minced
- 1 (1-inch) piece peeled fresh ginger, minced
- 1 Thai or serrano chili, seeded and finely diced
- 3 tablespoons fresh lime juice
- 1 tablespoon Asian fish sauce
- 1 tablespoon packed light brown sugar
- 2 tablespoons minced shallot
- ¾ pound carrots, peeled and julienned (about 3½ cups)
- 1 cup unsalted raw cashew pieces
- 2 teaspoons melted unrefined coconut oil
- ¼ teaspoon salt
- 1 lime
- ½ cup finely shredded unsweetened coconut
- Torn fresh cilantro leaves, for garnish
- Torn fresh mint leaves, for garnish

Preheat the oven to 350°F.

Use a mortar and pestle to grind the garlic, ginger, and chili into a paste, adding one ingredient at a time and being sure each is thoroughly ground before adding the next. Transfer the paste to a medium bowl. Add the lime juice, fish sauce, and brown sugar, and whisk to incorporate. Add the shallot and let the dressing sit for 5 minutes so the flavors can marry.

Add the carrots to the dressing and stir to combine. Set aside while you prepare the rest of the salad, stirring occasionally to help the carrots absorb as much flavor as possible.

In a small bowl, toss the cashews with the coconut oil. Add the salt and toss again. Zest the lime six or seven times over the nuts, and give a final toss to incorporate. Arrange the cashews on a baking sheet and toast, tossing halfway through, until fragrant, about 9 minutes. Transfer to a small bowl.

Arrange the coconut on a baking sheet in an even layer and toast it, tossing halfway through, until it releases its aroma and begins to turn golden, about 5 minutes. Remove the coconut from the oven.

Toss the carrots once more, then drain. Add the toasted coconut and toss to coat. Add the cashews and toss again to incorporate. Garnish with torn cilantro and mint.

Spending quality time with a cast-iron skillet, as I've done, has a few side effects. One is a recurring, uncontrollable urge to make upside-down cakes, and not the usual kind with pineapple. No. These cakes I have felt compelled to make are inverted and perverted. Forget the French tarte tatin or the latest highfalutin options like peach or quince. I drove right past rhubarb into the thick of the vegetable patch and kept going. I thought it might be fun to revisit carrot cake as we know it and use the defining ingredient as a topping instead of incorporating it into the batter. Once I tasted those caramelized carrots—and the cashews that accompany them—I knew it was more than fun; it was a revelation.

CARROT UPSIDE-DOWN CAKE

serves 12 to 14

TOPPING

- 7 or 8 medium carrots, peeled and sliced into ¼-inch-thick coins (2⅓ to 2½ cups)
- 1 cup plus 2 tablespoons coconut sugar
- 3 ounces unsweetened pineapple juice
- 6 tablespoons (¾ stick) unsalted butter
- ¾ teaspoon salt
- ¾ teaspoon orange zest
- 1 cup unsalted raw cashew pieces, toasted

CAKE

- 8 tablespoons (1 stick) unsalted butter, softened
- ½ cup unrefined coconut oil
- ⅔ cup coconut sugar
- ⅔ cup packed dark brown sugar
- 3 large eggs
- 1 teaspoon vanilla extract
- 2 cups all-purpose flour
- 1⅛ teaspoons ground cardamom
- 1 teaspoon baking powder
- ¼ teaspoon baking soda
- ½ teaspoon salt
- ⅔ cup whole milk
- 1 cup finely shredded unsweetened coconut

Vanilla or coconut ice cream, crème fraîche, or unsweetened whipped cream, for serving

(recipe continues)

Make the topping. Bring a large pot of water to a boil. Add the carrots and blanch them just until their color has brightened, about 2 minutes. Drain and quickly run the carrots under cold water to stop the cooking. Pat dry with paper towels.

Heat a 12-inch cast-iron skillet on the stove, gradually increasing the heat from low to medium. Add the coconut sugar, pineapple juice, butter, and salt to the pan, stirring to combine. When the butter and sugar have melted together, add the carrots and cook, stirring frequently, until the sauce is reduced by about half and turns a glossy, dark, tawny caramel color, about 15 minutes. Remove the skillet from the heat and stir in the orange zest and cashews to coat. Use a wooden spoon to spread the mixture into an even layer. Let it cool in the skillet. It will continue to thicken up a bit.

Preheat the oven to 350°F.

Make the cake. In the bowl of a stand mixer fitted with the paddle, combine the softened butter and coconut oil. Starting at a slow speed and increasing to medium-high, quickly beat them together until incorporated and smooth. Add the coconut and dark brown sugars, and continue to beat until the

mixture takes on a sludgy consistency, 3 to 5 minutes. Scrape down the sides of the bowl with a rubber spatula as needed. Add the eggs, one at a time, beating each to incorporate. Add the vanilla and mix to combine.

In a medium bowl, whisk together the flour, cardamom, baking powder, baking soda, and salt.

Gradually add the dry ingredients, then the milk, to the batter, mixing them on low speed and scraping down the sides of the bowl as needed. Add the shredded coconut and mix just to incorporate. You may want to give the batter a final folding or two with a rubber spatula to ensure the coconut is distributed throughout.

Using an offset spatula, carefully spread the batter over the carrots and cashews. Bake, rotating the skillet halfway through, until a tester inserted into the center comes out clean, about 40 minutes.

Let the cake cool in the skillet for 15 minutes before carefully unmolding it while it's still warm. Use a butter knife to loosen the sides from the pan, then invert it onto a plate. Slice it into 12 to 14 wedges and serve it with ice cream.

Whatever your stance on carnivorism, you've got to admire the resourcefulness of vegetarians and vegans who find workarounds for traditional recipes. Consider this my thank-you to them for introducing me to the secret lives of nuts, reminding me that coconut milk shouldn't be treated as an "ethnic" entity and left on the token "world cuisine" shelves of the grocery store (nothing should, really), and initiating me into the cult of coconut oil. Not just for carrots, this recipe works with sweet potato, pumpkin, and a host of winter squashes. The toppings for the roasted vegetable—whichever you choose—should be made in advance: the cream's cashews require an overnight soak, and the spiced nuts need to cool completely.

CURRY-ROASTED CARROTS
WITH CASHEW-COCONUT CREAM

serves 4

CASHEW-COCONUT CREAM

- 1 cup raw unsalted cashews, soaked overnight and drained
- ¾ cup full-fat unsweetened coconut milk
- ¼ teaspoon salt, plus more to taste

SPICED CASHEWS

- 1½ cups raw cashews
- ½ teaspoon nigella seeds (optional)
- ½ teaspoon coriander seeds
- 1 tablespoon melted unrefined coconut oil
- 1 teaspoon maple syrup
- ¼ teaspoon salt

CARROTS

- 3 pounds carrots, trimmed
- 3 tablespoons melted unrefined coconut oil
- 2 teaspoons medium-hot curry powder
- ¾ teaspoon salt
- ½ teaspoon freshly ground black pepper
- ¼ cup roughly chopped fresh cilantro
- ¼ cup roughly chopped fresh flat-leaf parsley
- 1 teaspoon pomegranate molasses

SUBSTITUTION NOTE Instead of pomegranate molasses, you can drizzle balsamic vinegar (ideally, an aged varietal) or Balsamic Syrup (page 199), adding more or less to your taste.

Make the cashew-coconut cream. Place the cashews in a food processor or blender and pulse a few times. With the motor running, drizzle in the coconut milk, stopping a few times to scrape down the sides. Transfer the cream to a small bowl and season with the salt, adjusting the amount to your taste and stirring to combine. Store in a sealed container in the fridge for up to 4 days.

Make the spiced cashews. Preheat the oven to 350°F. Line a baking sheet with parchment paper.

Spread out the raw cashews on the baking sheet. Bake, stirring occasionally, until toasted and fragrant, about 10 minutes.

Meanwhile, heat a large cast-iron skillet on the stove, gradually increasing the heat from low to medium-high. Add the nigella seeds, if using, and toast, shaking the skillet continuously until very fragrant, 1 to 2 minutes. Transfer them to a mortar, then toast the coriander seeds the same way (about 2 minutes), also adding them to the mortar. Give the seeds a few minutes to cool, then using a pestle, grind them together.

In a small bowl, stir together the coconut oil and maple syrup. Add the ground spice mix and salt, and stir to incorporate. When the cashews have finished their initial toasting, remove them from the oven, leaving it on, and add them to the bowl. Toss to coat evenly. Return the cashews to the parchment-lined sheet and bake until aromatic, 15 minutes more. Let the nuts cool completely, so they can crisp up, about 30 minutes. Store in an airtight container at room temperature for up to a week.

Prepare the carrots. Preheat the oven to 425°F. In a large bowl, toss the carrots with the coconut oil to coat. In a small bowl, combine the curry powder, salt, and pepper. Continue to toss the carrots as you sprinkle the spice mixture over them to coat evenly. Spread the carrots out onto a baking sheet and roast until cooked through and beginning to soften, up to 1 hour (or longer for larger carrots or if you like them extra soft).

Meanwhile, roughly chop 1 cup of the spiced roasted cashews. (Save the rest for snacking.)

Evenly divide the hot carrots among 4 bowls or plates. Top each portion with 2 generous spoonfuls of cashew-coconut cream (or more, if you'd like), 1 tablespoon each of the chopped cilantro and parsley, and one-fourth of the chopped spiced cashews. Drizzle ¼ teaspoon pomegranate molasses over each serving to finish.

SWEET POTATO

+ TAHINI

+ VANILLA

The sugar in starchy yams and the slight bitterness of spreadable sesame paste are highly—and alluringly—compatible. When they're paired in a savory preparation, vanilla comes in as a sultry, sophisticated surprise; when, less expectedly, they're combined in something sweet, that spice casts a soothing, almost nostalgic spell over them.

	CHARACTER	SUBSTITUTE	TIP	COMPLEMENTS
SWEET POTATO	Sweet, starchy, tuberous	Winter squash, potato, carrot	Everybody knows if it can be done to a potato, you can do it to a sweet potato.	Coconut, lime, leeks, onions, dates, maple syrup, cashews, almonds, hazelnuts, pecans, pumpkin seeds, bacon, duck, lamb
TAHINI	Nutty, bitter, smooth	Peanut butter	Occasionally flip the jar to prevent the oil from separating, or stir well before using.	Carrots, eggplant, spinach, figs, dates, chickpeas, salmon, lamb, harissa, dark chocolate
VANILLA	Warm, musky, floral	Anise, cardamom, nutmeg	1 bean = 1 teaspoon extract; scraped-out beans stored in sugar yield vanilla sugar.	Rhubarb, stone fruit, grapefruit, parsnip, fennel, heavy cream, brown butter, caramel, maple syrup, chocolate, nuts, lobster, scallop

I strongly believe sweet potato pie shouldn't be bound to the fixed set of aromatics that, rather unimaginatively, is the same used for pumpkin pie. So without overcomplicating things, I've flavored mine with vanilla and sesame, infusing them into both the filling and the crust. And what a crust! It's made with melted butter, and there's no rolling pin or chilling time necessary. I pilfered it from *The Back in the Day Bakery Cookbook* before adding sesame seeds and the scrapings of a vanilla bean. You'll probably like the flavor combo so much you'll wish you could do it with pumpkin. Good news: You can. The canned puree doesn't need to be boiled or beaten, and a little extra brown sugar should compensate for its lack of sweetness.

SWEET POTATO PIE

serves 8 to 10

FILLING

Salt

3 medium red-skinned sweet potatoes or yams, peeled and cut into 1-inch pieces

½ cup packed light brown sugar

½ teaspoon fine sea salt

4 tablespoons (½ stick) unsalted butter, softened

½ cup tahini

1 large egg

½ pint vanilla ice cream, melted (see Cooking Note)

CRUST

11 tablespoons (1 stick plus 3 tablespoons) unsalted butter

1 vanilla bean, split and scraped

1½ cups all-purpose flour

½ teaspoon fine sea salt

¼ cup packed light brown sugar

2 tablespoons toasted sesame seeds

Preheat the oven to 350°F and place a rack in the lower third.

Start the filling. Bring a large pot of water to a boil over high heat and lightly salt it. Add the sweet potatoes and cook until fork-tender, 10 to 13 minutes.

Meanwhile, make the crust. Melt the butter in a small saucepan over medium-low heat. Turn off the heat and add the scraped seeds from the split vanilla bean to the saucepan, swirling to incorporate. Let it sit on the stove, so the vanilla flavor permeates the butter, about 10 minutes.

In a medium bowl, whisk together the flour, fine sea salt, brown sugar, and sesame seeds. Slowly drizzle the vanilla-infused butter into the bowl, using a fork to incorporate the liquid, until the mixture is wet and crumbly. Using your fork or your hands, gather the dough into a large clump. Turn it out into an 8- or 9-inch pie dish and use your fingers to press the dough into the base and up the sides to create an even crust.

Finish the filling. Drain the sweet potatoes and transfer them to the bowl of a stand mixer fitted with the paddle. Beat on medium speed until smooth and creamy, scraping down the sides of the bowl with a rubber spatula as needed; you should have about 3 cups. Add the brown sugar, fine sea salt, and the butter, and beat on low speed to incorporate. Continuing to beat, add the tahini, followed by the egg. Scrape down the sides of the bowl. Finally, add the melted ice cream and beat again to incorporate. Transfer the filling into the pie shell, smoothing the top.

Bake the pie until the filling firms up, with the center remaining slightly jiggly, and the crust is golden brown, about 1 hour 15 minutes. Transfer the dish to a wire rack so the pie can cool completely. Chill in the refrigerator for at least 2 hours before serving.

COOKING NOTE The best way to halve a pint of ice cream is to use a serrated bread knife. Just saw the fresh-from-the-freezer container in two and peel off the carton wrapper.

One of the best things I've ever put in my mouth was a loaded white sweet potato at Superiority Burger, Brooks Headley's vegetarian restaurant in NYC's East Village. From its slit oozed a chunky green serrano-caper-tarragon salsa, soothed by a splat of labneh and decorated with a spray of pickles and a dribble of olive oil. *I can do that!* I thought. But I wanted to do it my own way, which, in general, is a highly pleasurable exercise that inevitably leads to new discoveries. I wondered, for example, if my tuber's "splat" could be a tahini-flavored cream, and found chef Alex Stupak's recipe for that very thing. I made my own version of that, too, of course. I'd apologize to Brooks and Alex if I didn't know I'd done good.

BAKED SWEET POTATOES
WITH TAHINI CREMA

serves 4

4 medium white sweet potatoes (see Substitution Note)

1 teaspoon sesame oil

¼ teaspoon salt, plus more to taste

¾ teaspoon freshly ground black pepper, plus more to taste

½ cup sour cream

¼ cup fresh lime juice

¼ cup tahini

1 vanilla bean, split and scraped

1 tablespoon unsalted butter

2 leeks, white and light green parts only, thinly sliced and rinsed well

1 tablespoon chopped fresh tarragon

Preheat the oven to 375°F.

Place each sweet potato on its own square of aluminum foil. Prick the potatoes all over a few times with a fork. Rub each with ¼ teaspoon sesame oil and sprinkle with a pinch of salt and a few grinds of fresh pepper. Seal each potato in its respective piece of foil and place them all together on a baking sheet. Cook the potatoes until the skin is crispy and the flesh is fork-tender, about 1 hour.

Meanwhile, in a small bowl, whisk together the sour cream, lime juice, ¼ cup water, the tahini, the scraped seeds from the vanilla bean, and ½ teaspoon of the pepper.

Melt the butter in a medium sauté pan over medium-high heat. Add the leeks, 1 teaspoon of the tarragon, ¼ teaspoon salt, and the remaining ¼ teaspoon pepper. Cook, stirring occasionally, until the leeks are soft and just beginning to brown, 7 to 9 minutes. Remove the pan from the heat.

To assemble, unwrap 1 sweet potato (see Cooking Note). Split it down the center, opening it up but leaving the halves connected. Spoon a few dollops of the tahini cream into the center of the potato and place one-fourth of the leeks on top. Garnish with some of the remaining chopped tarragon and sprinkle with salt to taste. Repeat with the remaining 3 potatoes. Serve hot, encouraging eaters to mash the toppings into the potato flesh so it gets creamy, kind of like mashed potatoes.

SUBSTITUTION NOTE White sweet potatoes are a bit starchier and more crumbly than yams, and they bake particularly well. But you can also use their orange-fleshed, red-skinned sweet counterparts.

COOKING NOTE Keep the baked sweet potato on its foil square while you split it open and dress it. Rewrap it, leaving the top open, and transfer it to a plate. It's a fun, tidy presentation that keeps the potatoes toasty.

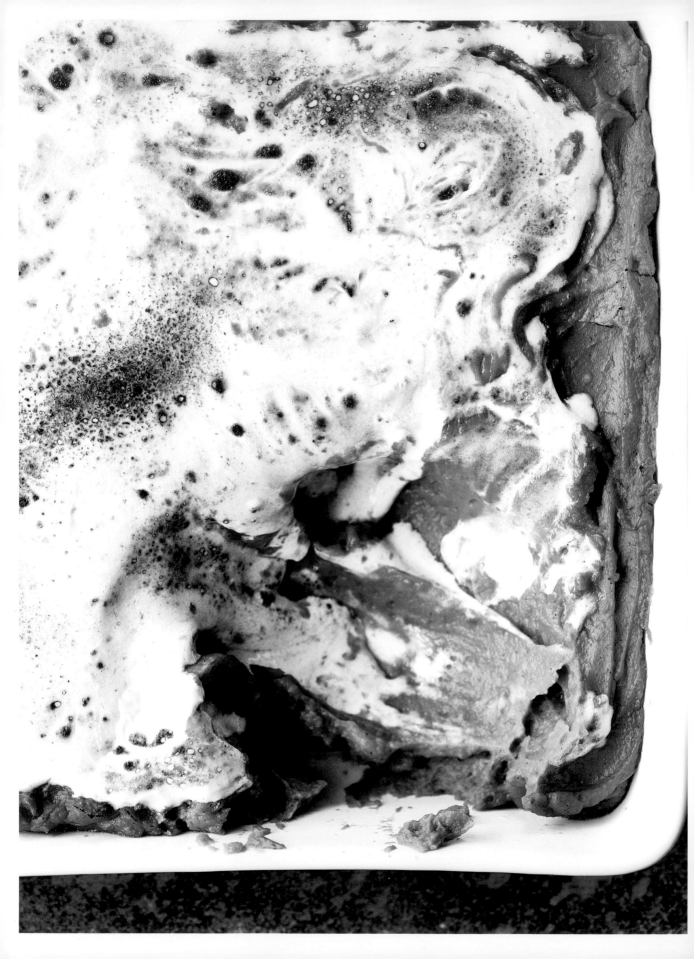

Sweet potato casserole is a Thanksgiving nonnegotiable. I wouldn't dare lobby to replace it. What I would do, though, is figure out how to make it without clinging to that Jet-Puffed marshmallow raft. The solution: Tahini Fluff. It's reminiscent of halva or nougat, and when baked at a high temperature for just a few minutes, it swells slightly and develops a thin, crisp, toasty crust with a soft, gooey layer beneath. Miso paste gives the yams a savory skew. Enriched with crème fraîche and vanilla-infused melted butter, the Fanta-colored mash is good enough to eat on its own. If you spread it into the baking dish and leave it in the fridge overnight, you can complete the recipe while you watch the Macy's parade.

SWEET POTATO CASSEROLE
WITH TAHINI FLUFF

serves 6 to 8

- 4 large or 5 medium red-skinned sweet potatoes or yams
- 8 tablespoons (1 stick) unsalted butter
- 1 vanilla bean, split and scraped
- ¼ cup plus 2 tablespoons crème fraîche (see Substitution Note)
- ¼ cup white miso paste
- ¾ teaspoon salt, plus more to taste
- 1 (7½-ounce) jar marshmallow spread
- ¼ cup plus 2 tablespoons tahini

Preheat the oven to 375°F.

Place the sweet potatoes on a foil-lined baking sheet and roast until very tender, 1¾ to 2 hours; the skin will crisp up and pull away from the mushy-soft flesh. Remove the sweet potatoes from the oven and let them cool slightly. Reduce the oven temperature to 350°F.

Meanwhile, melt the butter in a small saucepan over medium-low heat. Turn off the heat and add the scraped seeds from the split vanilla bean, swirling to incorporate. Let the mixture sit on the stove for 30 minutes to allow the vanilla flavor to permeate the butter.

In a small bowl, stir together the crème fraîche and miso paste.

When the potatoes are cool enough to handle, split them in half and peel the skin away from the flesh, discarding it. Transfer the flesh to a large bowl and mash it until smooth; you should have about 5 cups mashed sweet potato. Stir in the vanilla-infused butter, the crème fraîche–miso mixture, and ¼ teaspoon of the salt. Taste and adjust for salt as needed.

Transfer the mixture to an 8-inch square baking dish. Bake for 30 minutes, until heated through and the flavors have developed. Remove the baking dish from the oven and increase the temperature to 475°F.

In a medium bowl, combine the marshmallow spread, tahini, and the remaining ½ teaspoon salt. Using a rubber spatula, fold together to combine. Spread the mixture on top of the sweet potatoes. Bake until the tahini fluff has a lightly browned, toasted finish, about 7 minutes. Serve hot.

SUBSTITUTION NOTE If you don't have crème fraîche, use sour cream.

BEANS + GRAINS

CANNELLINI
+
GARLIC
+
CHILI

Nothing exemplifies Italy's Tuscan peasant cuisine better than creamy white beans slowly simmered with garlic, the stinking rose that's pungent and sweet. Shove some hot chili peppers into the pot and numerous countries could claim it. These three things are responsible for a diversity of nourishing dishes around the world.

	CHARACTER	SUBSTITUTE	TIP	COMPLEMENTS
CANNELLINI	Creamy, starchy, earthy	Alubi, Great Northern, navy, tarbais, Ayocote Blanco, flageolet, cranberry, pinto, runner, or Indian beans	Use dried and canned beans within 2 years.	Herbs, tomatoes, dark leafy greens, Parmesan, chicken stock, shellfish, tuna, pork belly, ham, sausage, lamb
GARLIC	Sharp, sweet, medicinal	Onions, shallots, scallions, Chinese chives, ramps, garlic scapes	When a recipe calls for mincing garlic, you can grate it instead of chopping it.	Vegetables, anchovies, pasta, potatoes, shellfish, poultry, meat
CHILI	Fiery, raisiny, smoky	Hot sauce, chili paste, chili oil, dried red chili flakes, cayenne pepper	Dried chili peppers last indefinitely. Fresh chilies can be refrigerated for up to 2 weeks.	Citrus, mango, watermelon, coconut, tomatoes, broccoli, eggplant, peanuts, tofu, seafood, poultry, meat, chocolate

A restorative simmer of beans is the ultimate example of cooking with pretty much nothing. It asks so little of your pantry or piggy bank. Soaking, you might be surprised to learn, is entirely optional. You must only promise not to pussyfoot around with your seasoning. My flavors here were inspired by a spice blend that combines smoked cinnamon with pimenton and garlic, and is meant to evoke the terroir of Catalonia. Turn your legumes into an even more filling dish with olive oil–embalmed anchovies, sardines, or tuna. Cooked sausage or shrimp are equally viable add-ons. Should you get bored (unlikely), omit the cinnamon and whole dried chilies, and swirl in a pesto blended with dried red chili flakes (see How to Pesto, page 139) for a fresh take.

A POT OF BEANS

serves 6

1 pound dried cannellini beans, rinsed

1 teaspoon salt, plus more to taste

2 tablespoons extra-virgin olive oil, plus more for serving

4 medium cloves garlic, peeled and lightly crushed

1 dried ancho chili pepper, stemmed and toasted (see page 66)

2 dried chipotle chilies, toasted

¼ teaspoon ground cinnamon

Rustic bread, sliced and toasted, for serving

Freshly ground black pepper to taste

OPTIONAL ADD-ONS

Olive oil–packed anchovies or sardines

Tuna conserved in olive oil

Merguez sausage or chorizo

Shrimp and thinly sliced red onion

Preheat the oven to 350°F.

Place the beans in a medium round Dutch oven (see Cooking Note) and add enough water to cover by 1 to 1½ inches. Add the salt, olive oil, garlic, chilies, and cinnamon, and bring to a boil over medium-high heat. Reduce the heat to medium-low to bring to a simmer, then cover and transfer to the oven. Bake until the beans are creamy and tender, 1½ to 2 hours; begin checking on them after 1 hour.

When the beans are done, discard the garlic and chilies. Taste and add as much salt as you like (about 1 teaspoon). Once cooled, the beans can be stored—in their cooking liquid—in a sealed container in the refrigerator for up to 1 week.

To serve, place a piece of toast at the bottom of a bowl. Ladle some of the beans on top with a bit of their broth. Splash with a glug of olive oil, crank a couple grinds of fresh pepper over them, and sprinkle with a pinch more salt to taste. Serve as is, or, if you like, with any of those add-ons stirred in or scattered on top.

COOKING NOTE I love to cook beans in my La Chamba, a Colombian black clay soup pot, because that material imparts extra smokiness. If you have a lidded clay pot, use it. Just make sure you've followed the manufacturer's instructions and seasoned it before cooking in it. Otherwise, a Dutch oven will deliver just fine

CHOOSING, TOASTING & GRINDING DRIED CHILIES

Combining a bunch of different peppers allows you to bring complexity to a dish. Think categorically: smoky, hot, and fruity. If your goal is to burn the roof off the house, use multiples of hot. The same is true if you want a pronounced smoky flavor to define a dish. If you want a balance of heat and smoke, use one from each of those groups.

Warning: Be careful when handling these peppers. They are powerful and can burn your skin. Unless you're working with a notably mild chili, always use kitchen gloves, and be mindful of your actions—don't rub your eyes or touch your face with those (covered) fingertips if they've been in contact with the fiery material.

Before toasting them, dust off your dried chilies with a damp paper towel. Larger ones should be stemmed and seeded—use a pair of clean kitchen scissors and work over a bowl to catch the detritus. For a longer chili with a smooth surface (like an Anaheim), cut off the stem and slit one of its edges so you can splay it, then scrape out the seeds and ribs. For larger, wrinkly chilies with inverted stems (like anchos), split the chili so you can turn it inside out and cut the stem out the way you core a fresh bell pepper, shaking any excess seeds into the bowl. If you're using them whole, smaller chilies (like arbol or Thai bird chilies) don't need to be seeded for toasting or grinding.

Toast chilies on the stove in a dry skillet over medium heat, using tongs to press them down against the surface of the pan and turn them as they cook, until they release their aroma and just begin to brown. They toast quickly, so be vigilant. Small chilies, like the chipotle, may take less than 1 minute per side, whereas their bigger relatives may require a bit more than that. Large batches can be roasted in the oven, spread out on baking sheets, at 350°F for about 5 minutes.

After you've toasted your chilies, you can grind them and use them as you would store-bought dried chili flakes. If you're planning to grind them, you should tear the larger dried chilies after stemming and seeding them (see above) and before toasting them. The small guys can be ground whole, seeds included. Use a spice grinder and blitz away. Just remember to let them cool before whizzing them.

Keep dried chili peppers in sealed, airtight containers in your pantry and use them within a year for optimal potency, or leave them in your freezer until you need them (within reason).

In the matter of *Refried Beans v. The Association of Culinary Misinformation*, we find the defendant guilty as charged. Regarding the dish in question, the word *refried* is a misnomer. The beans are being recooked, that's true. But it's their first fry! In Mexico, they'd be sizzled in lard; in America, rendered bacon fat. But I like to reach for butter and skip the part where I wait for my cured pork to surrender its grease. If you try it this way, you'll strengthen the comparison that's often made between this dish and mashed potatoes. (You'll also ingratiate yourself with vegetarians.) Blending your own chili powder is no big deal and makes a night-and-day difference in flavor. I'd be willing to prove it in a court of law . . . or in your kitchen.

RECOOKED BEANS

serves 4

2 tablespoons (¼ stick) unsalted butter

4 cloves garlic, peeled and gently crushed

2 (15-ounce) cans cannellini beans

Chili Powder (recipe follows)

½ teaspoon salt, plus more to taste

Juice of ½ lime

Lime zest (optional)

Heat a large cast-iron skillet on the stove, gradually increasing the heat from low to medium. Add the butter and, when it's foamy, add the garlic and cook until both sides are golden, 3 to 5 minutes total.

Add one can of beans and its liquid. Drain and rinse the second can, adding only the beans to the skillet. Add the chili powder. Mash the beans and the garlic together in the pan, combining them with the spice. Cook, mashing continuously, until they're mostly smooth but retain some texture, 10 to 12 minutes; when they're done, their liquid will have been incorporated. Turn off the heat and season with ½ teaspoon salt.

Transfer the beans to a serving bowl and stir in the lime juice. Taste again and, if needed, add a pinch more salt. If you want to amp up the brightness of the lime, garnish the beans with a few gratings of the zest. Eat it while it's hot!

CHILI POWDER

Makes about 1 tablespoon

1½ teaspoons cumin seeds, toasted and cooled

1 dried arbol chili pepper, stemmed, toasted, and cooled (see page 66)

¾ teaspoon dried oregano, preferably Mexican

In a spice grinder, combine the cumin, chili, and oregano, and grind into a blended powder. You can prepare this a few hours or even a couple of days in advance and store it in a sealed plastic bag until you need it. But it's best freshly made.

Ful or *ful medames* is Egypt's national dish of stewed fava beans seasoned with cumin seeds, garlic, a showering of lemon juice, and glugs of olive oil. Like fool's gold, this one isn't going to pass for the real thing. That doesn't mean you won't appreciate it for the creative riff it is. Many a valid version is spiked with chili flakes. I smuggle the heat into mine with a finishing oil, a condiment that can be dripped onto all sorts of things, like a slice of pizza or platter of roast potatoes. Serve ful with eggs—fried or hard-boiled—and pita for breakfast. That's how an Egyptian would do it, and in this instance, I see no reason to buck tradition.

FOOL'S FUL

serves 3 or 4

1 head of garlic

¾ cup plus 1 teaspoon extra-virgin olive oil

2 or 3 sprigs fresh oregano or marjoram, plus more for garnish

1½ teaspoons fennel seeds, toasted

2 (15-ounce) cans cannellini beans

1 tablespoon tahini

¼ cup fresh lemon juice (from about 2 lemons)

¾ teaspoon kosher salt, plus more to taste

Chili Oil (recipe follows or store-bought), to finish

Preheat the oven to 400°F.

Slice across the top of the head of garlic to expose the tips of the cloves. Place the head on a square of aluminum foil and drizzle 1 teaspoon olive oil over the exposed cloves. Add the oregano sprigs and wrap up the foil to create a sealed pouch. Place on a baking sheet and roast for 40 minutes, until the garlic is soft enough that you can squeeze the cloves into a small bowl.

Add the fennel seeds and a generous pinch of salt to the garlic and, using a fork, mash to form a paste.

Empty one can of beans, with its liquid, into a medium saucepan. Drain and rinse the second can, adding only the beans to the saucepan. Add the roasted garlic paste, the remaining ¾ cup olive oil, and the tahini, and stir to combine. Place the pan over medium-high heat and cook, stirring often, until the liquid begins to thicken, 5 to 7 minutes.

Add the lemon juice and salt, tasting and adjusting the salt as needed. If a thicker stew is desired, mash a third of the beans. Divide among 3 or 4 bowls, drizzle with some chili oil, and garnish generously with oregano leaves.

CHILI OIL

Makes 1 cup

1 cup extra-virgin olive oil

3 whole dried Calabrian chilies, stemmed

2 teaspoons dried red chili flakes

Heat 2 tablespoons of the olive oil in a small heavy-bottomed saucepan over medium heat. When the oil is shimmering, add the chilies and chili flakes, swirling the pan, until they release their aroma and start to sizzle, a matter of seconds. Watch closely; the chilies can burn quickly.

Add the rest of the oil to the pan, reduce the heat to low, and continue to cook just to warm the oil through, 2 to 3 minutes—it should be hot to the touch but not scalding; a thermometer inserted into the oil should read about 180°F. (If it's a bit hotter, don't worry.) Remove the pan from the heat and let the oil cool to room temperature, about 2 hours.

Transfer the cooled oil to a sealed airtight jar or bottle, leaving the chilies and chili flakes in it. Store it in the refrigerator for up to 6 months, letting it come to room temperature before using it.

ORECCHIETTE
+ BROCCOLI RABE
+ PINE NUTS

Although specific types have been identified in the following recipes, putting pasta, greens, and nuts together is the point—and always a win. Bouncy ear-shaped orecchiette are hidey-holes for morsels like sweet pine nuts, whose flavor carries a trace of evergreen. Broccoli rabe is a character-actor vegetable; it possesses a mustardy slap and tickle that straight-man broccoli does not.

	CHARACTER	SUBSTITUTE	TIP	COMPLEMENTS
ORECCHIETTE	Knobby, starchy, chewy	Cappelletti, cavatappi, cavatelli, conchiglie (small or medium), gemelli, pipette rigate, rocchetti, rotelle, rotini, campanelle, farfalle	Dried noodles take longer to cook than fresh. Remember to save some pasta cooking water.	Cauliflower, dark leafy greens, peas, sun-dried tomatoes, pesto, Parmesan, ricotta, nuts, shellfish, bacon, sausage
BROCCOLI RABE	Bitter, sharp, green	Mustard greens, Chinese broccoli, dandelion greens, kale, turnip greens, Swiss chard, broccoli, spinach	Boiling rabe before sautéing it removes bitterness. Don't eat it raw; do try roasting it.	Garlic, tomatoes, sun-dried tomatoes, sweet bell peppers, raisins, miso, black olives, anchovies, sausage, roast pork
PINE NUTS	Crunchy, buttery, resinous	Almonds, walnuts, hazelnuts, sunflower seeds, pistachios	Because they're high in oil, they go rancid quickly; smell to check for freshness.	Basil, sage, winter squash, roasted vegetables, salads, grains, ricotta, goat cheese, Parmesan, raisins, ground meat

These days, when I go to the kind of Italian-American restaurant affectionately referred to as a red sauce joint, first thing I do is scan the list of *contorni* (side dishes) for *rapini*. Sautéed in olive oil with loads of garlic, its acridness dissipates, and you're left with something that's more flavorful than spinach and fills the same dark-leafy-green quota. Dump it into a steaming bowl of pasta with Parmesan and pignoli and you've got a complete meal. Tiny troves of melted cheese and caramelized garlic nestle into the crevices of the orecchiette along with the pine nuts, revealing themselves as you dig in. For extra flavor and protein, add some chopped cured anchovies or cooked sausage to the rabe before tossing in the pasta.

ORECCHIETTE
WITH BROCCOLI RABE
serves 4

¼ cup extra-virgin olive oil

8 to 10 cloves garlic, finely sliced

1 pound fresh broccoli rabe, trimmed and roughly chopped

Juice of ½ lemon (optional)

Kosher salt to taste

Dried red chili flakes to taste

8 ounces dried orecchiette (about 2⅔ cups; see Substitution Note)

¼ cup pine nuts

⅓ cup grated Parmigiano-Reggiano, plus more for serving

Heat the olive oil and garlic together in a large pot over medium-high heat until fragrant, about 2 minutes. Add the broccoli rabe and give it a few stirs until the color brightens and it starts to wilt, 2 to 3 minutes. Add 1 cup water, cover the pan, and reduce the heat to low. Continue to cook, stirring from time to time, until it's soft and dulled in color a bit, 20 to 30 minutes. Drain and transfer to a medium bowl. Season with the lemon (if using), salt, and chili flakes.

Bring 3 quarts water to a boil in a large pot over high heat. When the water is boiling, salt it. Add the orecchiette, stirring once right after you put it in the pot and then again, a minute later, to prevent sticking. Cook it until al dente.

Meanwhile, toast the pine nuts. Heat a large sauté pan over medium-low heat. Add the nuts and cook, shaking constantly, for 3 to 4 minutes. As soon as they turn light brown and fragrant, turn off the heat. Add the cooked broccoli rabe, draining any residual liquid that may have pooled, and toss them together.

When the orecchiette is ready, drain it, reserving ½ cup of the pasta cooking water. Add the pasta and ¼ cup of the water to the pan with the pine nuts and rabe. Stir over medium heat to combine and coat the pasta. Add a tablespoon or two more of pasta water to loosen the sauce as needed. Stir in the cheese.

Divide among 4 bowls and serve with additional cheese on the side.

SUBSTITUTION NOTE Use whatever type of dried pasta you like best. I recommend shapes that can hold things in their curves or ridges. But spaghetti's always reliable; the broccoli rabe can be twirled up with the pasta strands.

I've always associated noodle casseroles with institutions where the food is notoriously bad—schools, hospitals, prisons. I imagine thick, congealed white cream sauce, and my stomach flinches. It doesn't have to be this way. Introducing an actually good one-pan pasta bake: it has crème fraîche, ricotta, and—drumroll, please—pine nut butter. [Pause for applause.] Lemon lightens the load, panko crumbs embellish with elegance, and scrappy broccoli rabe gives the dish just enough bite to rise above its station.

ACTUALLY GOOD NOODLE CASSEROLE

serves 4

1 head of garlic

1 teaspoon extra-virgin olive oil

8 ounces dried orecchiette (about 2⅔ cups)

1 pound broccoli rabe, trimmed

8 ounces crème fraîche (about ¾ cup)

½ cup fresh ricotta cheese

3 tablespoons Pine Nut Butter (recipe follows; see Substitution Note)

2 tablespoons whole milk

¼ teaspoon cayenne pepper

1¾ teaspoons kosher salt, plus more to taste

1 tablespoon unsalted butter, melted, plus more for greasing

1 cup panko crumbs

Zest and juice of ¼ lemon

Preheat the oven to 400°F. Grease a gratin pan or a 1- to 2-quart baking dish liberally.

Slice across the top of the head of garlic to expose the tips of the cloves. Place the head on a square of aluminum foil and drizzle the olive oil over the exposed cloves. Wrap up the foil to create a sealed pouch. Place on a baking sheet and roast for 40 minutes, until the garlic is soft enough that you can squeeze the cloves into a large bowl. Reduce the oven temperature to 375°F.

Meanwhile, bring 3 quarts water to a boil in a large pot over high heat. When the water is boiling, salt it. Add the orecchiette, stirring once right after you put it in the pot and then again, a minute later, to prevent sticking. Cook it until just shy of al dente. Reserving the pasta cooking water in the pot, strain the orecchiette and transfer it to a medium bowl. Return the water to a boil.

Add the broccoli rabe to the boiling water and cook for about 2 minutes, until just wilted and vibrant in color. Using tongs, remove the greens from the pot and rinse them under cold water. Use your hands (or paper towel) to squeeze out excess water, then roughly chop.

Using a fork or spoon, mash the garlic in the large bowl into a paste—don't worry if it's chunky. Add the crème fraîche and stir to incorporate. Add the ricotta, stirring again to combine. Add the pine nut butter, stirring to be sure all ingredients are distributed evenly and incorporated well. Stir in the milk to loosen the thick sauce a bit. Season with the cayenne and ¾ teaspoon of the salt.

Add the pasta to the sauce and, using a spatula, mix to coat. Add the rabe and stir again, being sure all ingredients are well dispersed. Taste and add more salt (about ½ teaspoon) as needed. Transfer the mixture to the prepared pan.

In a small bowl, combine the melted butter with the panko. Stir to mix. Add the lemon zest and ½ teaspoon salt, stirring to combine. Squeeze in the lemon juice and stir again. Sprinkle the topping over the pan, coating the entire surface as evenly as possible.

Bake the casserole until the top is golden and the sides are bubbling up, about 40 minutes, rotating the pan halfway through. Let the casserole sit for at least 10 minutes to set before digging in.

PINE NUT BUTTER
Makes 1 cup

½ pound pine nuts, toasted and
  cooled completely
1½ teaspoons neutral oil
1¼ teaspoons kosher salt

Place the cooled toasted nuts
in a food processor along with
the oil and salt. Process until
smooth. You can make this in
advance and store it in an airtight container in the refrigerator for up to 2 weeks.

SUBSTITUTION NOTE I encourage you to make the Pine Nut Butter. You could halve the recipe—the nuts are expensive—but this is a great condiment to have on hand. Try it in a sandwich, PB&J-style, or an open-face tartine, spreading it onto your toast and topping it with roasted vegetables. You can also put it into smoothies. To use it in a sweet application, like brownies or shortbread sandwich cookies, start with ¾ teaspoon salt and add more as needed. If you don't go this route, you will probably have decent success using store-bought almond butter (but you didn't hear that from me).

When the small, unpretentious Japanese restaurant in my neighborhood that I routinely ordered in from closed after twenty years, the loss felt personal. It was a reliable fixture, and the only place I knew that served what the menu listed as *yuba-ae*, sliced tofu skin ribbons (*yuba*) tangled up with broccoli rabe and dressed in a standout vinaigrette that tasted like a sharper, more savory honey mustard. The chewy soy-based strips aren't the easiest ingredient to find, so I replaced them with pasta. The owner was kind enough to disclose the dressing's two main components—miso and mustard—but smart enough to keep the rest a secret. I relied on my taste memory to figure it out. I think I nailed it.

PASTA SALAD
WITH MISO-MUSTARD DRESSING

serves 4

MISO-MUSTARD DRESSING

1 tablespoon Colman's mustard powder

3 tablespoons white miso paste

3 tablespoons unseasoned rice vinegar

1 tablespoon mirin

1 tablespoon sugar

1 tablespoon neutral oil

SALAD

8 ounces dried orecchiette (about 2⅔ cups; see Substitution Note)

1 pound broccoli rabe, trimmed

¼ cup plus 2 tablespoons pine nuts

Salt to taste

About 40 (3 × ½-inch) strips of toasted nori (optional)

Make the dressing. In a small bowl, mix the mustard powder with 2 teaspoons water to create a thick paste. Let it sit for 20 minutes to allow the flavor to develop. In a separate small bowl, using a whisk or fork, stir 1 teaspoon of the mustard paste with the miso paste, rice vinegar, mirin, and sugar to combine. Stir in the oil to incorporate thoroughly (see Cooking Note).

Prepare the salad. Bring 3 quarts water to a boil in a large pot over high heat. When the water is boiling, salt it. Add the orecchiette, stirring once right after you put it in the pot and then again, a minute later, to prevent sticking. Cook it until al dente. Reserving the pasta cooking water in the pot, strain the orecchiette and transfer it to a serving bowl. Return the water to a boil.

Prepare a large bowl of ice water. Add the broccoli rabe to the boiling water and cook for about 2 minutes, until it's just wilted and vibrant in color. Drain and immediately transfer it to the ice water to stop the cooking. Use your hands (or paper towel) to squeeze out excess water, then roughly chop. Add the rabe to the orecchiette.

Add the pine nuts and stir to combine with the orecchiette and rabe. Dress the salad with the miso-mustard mixture and toss to coat evenly. Season with salt. Garnish with the nori strips, if using. Before serving, toss again so the toasted seaweed wilts and scatters.

COOKING NOTE If you like your salads more heavily dressed, consider increasing the amounts for the white miso, rice vinegar, mirin, sugar, and oil by 50 percent. You will have enough mustard paste to accommodate a larger batch. The dressing can be refrigerated in an airtight container for up to a week.

SUBSTITUTION NOTE I strongly suggest orecchiette or shells here—small or medium size. Otherwise, for a rice-like texture, use orzo, or think beyond noodles and try it with brown rice.

ARBORIO RICE
+
ONION
+
PARMESAN

In the West, long-grain rice is the norm, but in Japan, medium length is always the first choice. The Italian equivalent, Arborio, is synonymous with risotto. Onions and Parmesan cheese are both sources of umami, one sweet, the other salty, respectively. Together, they endow the texturally satisfying, bland starch with maximum flavor.

	CHARACTER	SUBSTITUTE	TIP	COMPLEMENTS
ARBORIO RICE	Starchy, creamy, medium grain	Carnaroli rice, white sushi rice, Bomba rice, farro, pearled barley, Israeli couscous	Arborio, or any medium-grain rice, yields creamier rice pudding.	Stock, wine, pesto, saffron, asparagus, green peas, mushrooms, winter squash, pine nuts, shellfish, bone marrow
ONION	Sweet, pungent, astringent	Shallots, leeks, chives, scallions	Soak sliced raw red onions in ice water for 15 minutes to make them milder.	Mushrooms, figs, stinky or salty cheeses, bacon, sausage, roasted meat and chicken, calves' and chicken livers
PARMESAN	Sharp, nutty, hard	Grana Padano, Pecorino Romano, Asiago, aged Gouda	Aged Parmigiano-Reggiano from Emilia-Romagna is the real thing; *Parmesan* is the generic term.	Soups, vegetables, pasta, potatoes, arugula, chicories, romaine, garlic, anchovies, chicken

Many a risotto begins with heating onions in a pan. From there, the rice goes in, followed by the featured ingredients—peas and prosciutto, wild mushrooms, butternut squash, or saffron. But what if your risotto were to start *and* end with those onions? Stripping the dish down to its fundamentals gets you one stunningly rich bowl of rice. A spoonful of white miso, an unexpected guest at this Italian affair, doubles the onion's savory potency. Then, Parmesan comes along and triples it. I replace the standard white wine with Japanese sake so that the fermented soybean paste has some familiar company.

ONION RISOTTO

serves 4 to 6

- 3 cups finely chopped yellow onions (2 to 3 medium onions), skins and scraps reserved
- 5 cups vegetable stock
- Parmesan rind (optional; see Cooking Note)
- 4 tablespoons (½ stick) unsalted butter
- 2 tablespoons extra-virgin olive oil
- 2 cups Arborio rice (see Substitution Note)
- 1 cup sake (or dry white wine)
- 1 tablespoon white miso paste
- ½ cup freshly grated Parmesan cheese, plus more for serving
- ¼ cup finely chopped fresh flat-leaf parsley
- ½ teaspoon salt, plus more to taste
- ¼ teaspoon freshly ground black pepper, plus more to taste

Place the onion skins and scraps in a medium saucepan with the vegetable stock and bring to a simmer over high heat. Add the Parmesan rind (if using), and reduce the heat to low to maintain the simmer as you continue cooking.

Heat 2 tablespoons of the butter and the olive oil together in a large sauté pan over medium heat. When the butter is melted and combined with the oil, add the chopped onions and cook, stirring frequently, until soft and fragrant, 5 to 7 minutes. Add the rice and cook, continuing to stir, until it takes on a pearly, opaque cast, 3 to 5 minutes. Add the sake and simmer until the alcohol evaporates. Stir in the miso.

Stirring continuously, add enough simmering stock (reserving the solids in the pan) to cover the rice and cook, letting the grains soak up enough liquid so the top of the rice is just visible above it. Add more stock to cover and cook, waiting until the liquid has been absorbed and the top of the rice appears before adding more stock to cover again. Repeat this process, stirring continuously, until you've used most of the stock and the rice is tender with an al dente bite. The risotto will have a creamy texture, but the rice itself should not be mushy.

Stir in the remaining 2 tablespoons butter, the Parmesan, and the parsley. Add the salt and pepper, taste, and adjust the seasoning to your liking. Serve immediately with extra grated cheese on the side.

COOKING NOTE Enriching a simmering soup or stew with cheese rinds is an old practice that makes flavorful use of what would otherwise be treated as garbage. Store them in a zip-top bag in your freezer and plop them in your pot of soup as it nears the end of its cooking time, or, alternatively, when you're reheating it, just before serving. Discard after using.

SUBSTITUTION NOTE Play up the use of Japanese ingredients in this risotto by swapping in that country's medium-grain rice.

I was thinking of arancini, the fried snacks formed from the previous day's risotto, when I plotted this recipe. But it's not as if Italy has a monopoly on repurposing rice this way; in India you'll find crispy *pakora*, and in New Orleans, sweet-battered Creole calas, both made with the precooked grains. Since no country can claim them, I gave my balls a nonspecific name. With a drizzle of honey and a flick of chili flakes, these fritters are a reward for a rough day at school and also do well as party hors d'oeuvres. I recommend them with a bowl of Broccoli Leek Soup (page 35) for lunch. Before you race off to your kitchen to heat the oil, a word: the fritters should be refrigerated for at least an hour before frying.

RICE FRITTERS

makes 17 fritters

- 3 cups beef or chicken stock
- 1 dried bay leaf
- 5 sprigs fresh thyme, tied together with kitchen twine
- 1 cup Arborio rice
- ⅔ teaspoon sugar
- 1½ medium yellow onions
- 1 teaspoon unsalted butter
- Pinch of baking soda
- ⅓ teaspoon kosher salt, plus more to taste
- A few grinds of freshly ground black pepper
- ¾ cup grated Parmesan cheese
- 1½ teaspoons finely chopped fresh flat-leaf parsley
- 2 large eggs
- 1⅓ cups bread crumbs
- 17 (½-inch) cubes Gruyère cheese (about ½ cup)
- Neutral oil, for frying

Combine the stock, bay leaf, and thyme in a medium saucepan over medium-high heat. Bring to a boil. Stir in the rice, then reduce the heat to medium-low and simmer until the grains are tender and the liquid has been absorbed, about 20 minutes. Discard the bay leaf and thyme. Spread the cooked rice on a parchment-lined baking sheet and let cool completely, about 1 hour.

Meanwhile, heat the sugar in a medium stainless-steel skillet over medium-high heat until completely melted and light brown, shaking and swirling the pan occasionally to prevent sticking or burning, about 4 minutes. Add the onions and, using a wooden spoon, stir them to coat in the melted sugar. Add the butter, baking soda, salt, and pepper. Stir to combine. Cook, shaking the pan occasionally, until the onions release all their liquid and a brown coating builds up on the bottom, 6 to 8 minutes.

Add 2 tablespoons water to the onions and scrape up the browned bits from the bottom of the skillet. Continue cooking, shaking occasionally, until the coating begins to build up again, 3 to 5 minutes. Repeat the loosening and cooking steps three or four more times until the onions are deep brown. Transfer the mixture to a small bowl and allow to rest at room temperature for 5 minutes.

Combine ¼ cup of the grated Parmesan and the parsley in a small bowl; set aside.

Beat the eggs in a large bowl, then stir in the cooled rice, caramelized onions, the remaining ½ cup Parmesan, and ⅔ cup of the bread crumbs to combine. With damp hands, scoop up about 3 tablespoons of the mixture and round it in your palm. Using the thumb of your other hand, make a depression in the center of the rice and sprinkle in about 1 teaspoon of the parsley-Parmesan mixture. Place a cube of Gruyère on top of it, pushing the cheese into the rice and closing the rice mixture around it to cover the filling completely, and shape it to form a ping-pong-ball-size sphere, about 1½ inches in diameter. Repeat with the remaining mixture to make 17 balls.

Place the remaining ⅔ cup bread crumbs in a shallow bowl or small baking dish. Roll the balls through the bread crumbs and place them on a parchment lined baking sheet. Cover loosely with plastic wrap or aluminum foil and refrigerate at least 1 hour or overnight.

Heat 3 inches of oil in a large saucepan over medium-high heat until a deep-fry thermometer registers 350°F. Working in batches, fry the rice balls, turning, until golden brown on all sides, about 4½ minutes. Remove with a slotted spoon and drain on paper towels. Season with salt, if needed. Let cool, slightly, and serve while still hot.

Of all the things you can do with leftover rice, turning it into a piecrust is probably the coolest. Bound with an egg white and some Parmesan cheese, it begins to take on the consistency of dough. As someone who always manages to dribble batter in her wake, I appreciate this crust for being forgivingly messproof; if anything, it welcomes spills. Should any of the filling accidentally slosh out as you pour it in, the rice mixture will absorb it in the oven and become crispier for it. You can use the base for any savory tart; just change the cheese and seasonings to match. Similarly, you can pour the creamy custard teeming with onions into a pastry shell and call it a quiche.

ONION TART

makes one 8- or 9-inch tart

- 1½ cups packed cooked Arborio rice
- 2 teaspoons salt, plus more to taste
- 1 teaspoon freshly ground black pepper, plus more to taste
- 1 tablespoon plus 1 teaspoon finely chopped fresh sage
- ½ cup plus 1 tablespoon grated Parmesan cheese
- 1 large egg white
- 8 tablespoons (1 stick) unsalted butter, plus more for greasing
- 5 medium yellow onions, thinly sliced (about 9 cups)
- 5 large egg yolks
- 1 cup heavy cream

Preheat the oven to 425°F. Grease an 8- or 9-inch metal pie pan or cake pan.

In a large bowl, combine the rice, ½ teaspoon of the salt, ¼ teaspoon of the pepper, the sage, and the cheese. Add the egg white and mix well to incorporate; the mixture should hold together when you press it in your palms.

Press the rice evenly into the prepared pan. As you push it into the pan, it will start to resemble a dough. Place the pan on a baking sheet and parbake to set the crust, 10 to 12 minutes. Remove it from the oven and let cool completely, about 45 minutes. Reduce the oven temperature to 350°F. Within 2 hours of baking it, the prepared crust can be wrapped in plastic and stored in the refrigerator overnight; let it come to room temperature before proceeding.

Melt the butter in a large sauté pan over medium-low heat. Add the onions and sprinkle with ¾ teaspoon of the salt, giving them a quick, gentle stir. Cover and cook, being sure they

don't take on any color. (If they begin to, reduce the heat.) As they sweat, they should release a noticeable amount of liquid. When they're soft and sloshy, after about 30 minutes, uncover and continue to cook them, stirring occasionally, until almost all of the liquid has evaporated, about 1 hour more. Transfer the onions and any remaining liquid to a large bowl to cool. The onions will keep in an airtight container in the refrigerator for up to 5 days.

In a medium bowl, whisk together the egg yolks and cream. Add the mixture to the bowl with the onions, whisking to incorporate. Add the remaining ¾ teaspoon salt and ¾ teaspoon pepper. Taste and adjust for seasoning.

Carefully pour the onion mixture into the cooled crust, filling it as high as you can without overflowing; you will likely have some left over and can discard it. Bake until the filling is set and the top is lightly browned, 40 to 45 minutes. Let cool for at least 30 minutes before slicing and serving.

LONG-GRAIN RICE
+
CHINESE SAUSAGE
(LAP CHEONG)
+
EGG

Can you think of a rice-free cuisine? Me neither. Eggs are just as pervasive and can bind the rice, create a wrapper for the nutty grain, or be scattered throughout. Conversely, *lap cheong*, or Chinese sausage, is geographically specific. The sweet, larded, fermented stuff makes those other two ingredients taste less generic.

	CHARACTER	SUBSTITUTE	TIP	COMPLEMENTS
LONG-GRAIN RICE	Toasty, fluffy, nonsticky	Quinoa, barley, orzo; nonwhite rice (brown, black, red, purple)	1 cup raw rice yields about 3 cups cooked. Rinsing dry rice reduces its stickiness.	Spicy foods, stews, stir-fries, curries; herbs, spices, scallions, ginger, beans, coconut, butter, ghee, almonds, chicken
CHINESE SAUSAGE	Sweet, funky, dried	Chicken-and-apple sausage, bacon, merguez, chorizo (Note: These aren't as sweet.)	Keep this at room temperature for a few weeks or in an airtight container in the fridge or freezer for months.	Fresh herbs, soy sauce, maple syrup, onions, black pepper, chestnut, winter squash, sweet potato, shellfish
EGG	Versatile, rich, binding	Egg replacers, silken tofu, ground flaxseed, applesauce, mashed banana (for baking)	Eggs are easier to separate when cold and best beaten at room temperature.	Soy sauce, hot sauce, ketchup, fresh herbs, onions, scallions, mushrooms, asparagus, noodles, miso, caviar, pork

In China, people often start—and finish—the day with congee. It's an all-the-time-everywhere comfort food. Some version of the savory rice-based porridge exists in countries throughout Asia; the seasonings and add-ons change from one locale to the next, but the soupy foundation stays the same. You can look at each steaming bowlful as a catchall for many of your favorite ingredients. I stir an egg into mine for extra silkiness. The toppings are where it gets personal (and fun). I think everyone should garnish everything with French's fried onions, but it's your congee; you make the call.

CONGEE
WITH ALL THE FIXINGS

serves 4

1 cup uncooked jasmine rice (see Substitution Note)

1 (2-inch) piece peeled fresh ginger

8 cups chicken stock, plus more as needed

Salt to taste

2½ links dried Chinese sausage, casing removed and roughly chopped

1 clove garlic, minced

2 whole scallions, thinly sliced, dark green parts separate

Dried red chili flakes to taste (optional)

4 large eggs

Ground white pepper to taste

Juice of 1 lime

French's Crispy Fried Onions, for garnish

Using a sieve, rinse the rice under cold water until the water runs clear. Place the rice in a medium to large saucepan along with the ginger and 8 cups chicken stock. Bring the liquid to a boil over high heat, then reduce the heat to medium-low and simmer for at least 1 hour, stirring occasionally. If the porridge looks stiff or dry during cooking, add more stock, ½ to 1 cup at a time. It's ready when the rice is on the brink of falling apart and resembles porridge. If you like it looser, add more stock. Taste and season with salt as needed.

When your congee looks almost finished, heat a large cast-iron skillet on the stove, gradually increasing the heat from low to medium. Add the sausage and sauté, stirring occasionally, until it's crisp and the fat has been rendered, about 5 minutes. Add the garlic, white and light green scallion slices, and a pinch of chili flakes (if using), sautéing them with the sausage until the scallions are tender, stirring frequently, 3 to 4 minutes. Remove the skillet from the heat.

Ladle the congee into 4 bowls and, while it's piping hot, crack an egg into each, stirring it in so it cooks in the porridge. Spoon some of the sausage mixture, fat included, into each bowl, and season each with a pinch of white pepper and some lime juice. Garnish each bowl with the dark green scallion slices and as many fried onions as you like.

> **SUBSTITUTION NOTE** This recipe will work with a long- or short-grain rice; I prefer congee made with white rice, but any color will do.

I discovered the miracle of crunchy rice through a Persian specialty known as *tah dig*, or the golden, crackle-pop crust of rice formed in the bottom of a pan. The crispy-to-shattering caramelized layer beneath the mound of fluffy grains is the calling card of a good home cook in that region. You'll find similar pot-sticking practices beyond Iran—in Spain, Thailand, and Senegal, to name a few. My version of this "rice brittle" (a term I'm submitting to whichever official committee presides over culinary nomenclature) is a coconutty multicultural mishmash, from its toasty bottom to its gooey fried-egg top.

CRUNCHY COCONUT RICE

serves 4

- 1 (13½-ounce) can full-fat unsweetened coconut milk
- 1¼ cups finely shredded unsweetened coconut
- 1½ cups uncooked basmati rice
- 2 teaspoons salt, plus more to taste
- 3½ links dried Chinese sausage, casing removed and sliced into ¼-inch-wide rounds
- 6 whole black peppercorns
- 3 green cardamom pods, lightly crushed
- 3 tablespoons melted unrefined coconut oil
- 8 teaspoons unsalted butter
- 4 large eggs
- Freshly ground black pepper to taste
- Up to ½ cup unseasoned rice vinegar (see Cooking Note)
- Fresh cilantro leaves, for garnish

Heat about half of the coconut milk in a small saucepan over low-medium until steam begins to rise off the surface. Stir in the coconut and set it aside to rehydrate for 30 minutes. Strain the coconut through a sieve set over a medium bowl. Place the flakes in a small bowl and reserve the steeped coconut milk.

Meanwhile, using a clean sieve, rinse the rice under cold water until the water runs clear. In a medium pot, bring 6 cups water to a boil over high heat. Add 1 teaspoon of the salt and the rinsed rice, and cook until the centers of the grains just start to look chalky, about 5 minutes. Drain and set aside.

Heat a large cast-iron skillet on the stove, gradually increasing the heat from low to medium-low. Add the sausage and sauté just until its edges are beginning to crisp, stirring occasionally, about 5 minutes. Add the peppercorns and cardamom pods, and toast until aromatic, about 2 minutes. Add the reserved coconut flakes and sauté, stirring occasionally, until fragrant, 3 to 5 minutes. Add the reserved rice, remaining 1 teaspoon salt, 3 tablespoons of the reserved steeped coconut milk, and the coconut oil. Stir to incorporate, then spread the mixture evenly across the skillet; using the handle of a wooden spoon, poke holes into the surface of the rice to allow steam to escape. Cover the skillet and increase the heat to medium. Cook for 10 minutes.

Add all of the remaining coconut milk (both steeped and still in the can). Place a clean kitchen towel under the lid to catch the condensation, put the lid back on the pan, and reduce the heat to medium-low. Cook the rice until it starts to smell nutty or sounds like gently popping corn, 40 minutes or so; check it at 30 minutes to see how the crust is progressing by lifting the rice from the skillet with a spatula. Rotate the pan around the flame every 10 minutes as the rice cooks, shifting it occasionally for even crisping and to avoid burning. Remove the skillet from the heat and let it sit, covered, for 10 minutes.

Meanwhile, in a medium skillet over medium heat, melt 2 teaspoons of the butter. When the butter is sizzling, crack 2 of the eggs into the skillet and fry until their whites are cooked through and the yolks are barely set, 2 to 3 minutes. Transfer the eggs to a plate and sprinkle each with a pinch of salt and a couple grinds of pepper. Repeat with 2 more teaspoons of the butter and the remaining 2 eggs.

Melt the remaining 4 teaspoons butter in the same skillet over medium heat. When the foaming subsides, add the vinegar and a generous pinch or two more of salt, swirling the skillet to incorporate; it will bubble up and hiss. When a sauce forms and reduces slightly, 3 to 4 minutes, remove the skillet from the heat.

Stir the rice up from the bottom of its pan, incorporating the crunchy crust into the rest, discarding the peppercorns and cardamom pods. Evenly divide the rice among 4 bowls, slide an egg on top of each, and pour a couple of spoonfuls of the sauce over the top. Garnish with fresh cilantro to your taste. Serve immediately.

COOKING NOTE I like a bright, acidic, vinegar-forward sauce here, and unseasoned rice vinegar is the mildest option, so I add a full ½ cup. You can use less or try something sharper like red wine, sherry, apple cider, or Chinese black vinegar.

Next time you order Chinese food for delivery, don't throw out that extra carton of rice they give you. You can make omelets with it. I definitely thought this was a screwy-sounding idea until I tried it. *Omuraisu*, as the dish is called, is Japanese home cooking at its best. You dump the leftover starch in a hot pan, as you would for fried rice, season it with a salty-sweet sauce you'll want to bottle, then fold it all up in a thin, fluffy egg wrapper. The filling can be made with any day-old cooked rice and enjoyed on its own, but I encourage you to follow the recipe through to the end: I promise this omelet is a bundle of joy.

RICE OMELET

serves 4

¼ cup white miso

2 tablespoons maple syrup

1 tablespoon ketchup

1 tablespoon soy sauce

2½ links dried Chinese sausage, casing removed and roughly chopped

1 small yellow or sweet onion, finely chopped

2 cups cooked rice

Freshly ground black pepper to taste

2 tablespoons roughly chopped fresh basil, plus more for garnish

6 large eggs

4 tablespoons crème fraîche

Salt to taste

8 teaspoons neutral oil

Roughly chopped fresh flat-leaf parsley, for garnish

Heat the miso, maple syrup, ketchup, and soy sauce together in a small saucepan over medium-low heat, stirring constantly to combine, until smooth, 2 to 3 minutes. Watch closely, as it can burn quickly. Remove pan from the heat.

Heat a large cast-iron skillet on the stove, gradually increasing the heat from low to medium. Add the sausage and sauté, stirring occasionally, until it's crisp and the fat has been rendered, about 5 minutes. Add the onion and sauté just until soft and translucent, 5 to 7 minutes. Add the rice, using a wooden spoon to break it up, and combine the ingredients. Cook until heated through, 2 to 3 minutes, then stir in 3 tablespoons of the sauce to incorporate. Season with pepper. Transfer the rice to a medium bowl and stir in the basil.

In a medium bowl, lightly beat together the eggs, crème fraîche, and a generous pinch of salt and pepper. Transfer the mixture to a spouted measuring cup. Heat 2 teaspoons of the oil in an 8-inch skillet over medium-high heat. When the oil is shimmering, pour in one-fourth of the egg mixture (about ⅓ cup). As the eggs begin to set, tilt the pan toward you and, using a spatula, lift the edges of the omelet so any uncooked egg can run underneath. Next, tilt the pan away from you. Repeat this tilting and lifting, back and forth, until the omelet is set but still slightly runny on top, about 2 minutes. Remove the pan from the heat and gently slide the omelet out flat onto a plate. Line half of the omelet with one-fourth of the rice mixture, then fold the empty half over the filling to form a half-moon.

Repeat to make 3 more omelets, using the rest of the oil and egg-and-rice mixtures as above, and plating each separately. Wipe the pan clean between omelets. Drizzle some of the remaining sauce over each omelet, garnish with the fresh herbs, and serve.

OATS
+
APPLE
+
GOUDA

Some Americans have an affinity for apple pie with Cheddar; others think that's peculiar. Since fruit-and-cheese pairings aren't uncommon, it's probably the dessert-related circumstances that throw people off. But aged Gouda has brown-sugar undertones, which makes it a better fit for apples and a perfect one for oats, regardless of context.

	CHARACTER	SUBSTITUTE	TIP	COMPLEMENTS
OATS	Nutty, filling, absorbent, gluten-free	Buckwheat groats, millet, quinoa, amaranth, sorghum, brown rice, wild rice, farro, barley	Treat them like nuts—toast them to deepen their flavor; grind them for flour.	Brown sugar, maple, brown butter, olive oil, pesto, onions, nuts, roasted fruit or vegetables
APPLE	Crisp, sweet, tart	Pear, jicama, sweet potato, winter squash, parsnip, dried apple	Granny Smith, Pink Lady, Honeycrisp, and Jonagold are solid multipurpose varietals.	Fennel, cabbage, radicchio, carrot, ginger, almonds, pecans, walnuts, hazelnuts, Cheddar, Brie, Taleggio, Parmesan, smoked mozzarella
AGED GOUDA	Salty, butterscotch, crystalline	Romano, aged Cheddar, Parmesan, Comté	Enjoy it on its own or on a cheese plate. Sheep's milk Ewephoria is recommended.	Tomatoes, onions, leeks, pasta, potatoes, bread, bacon, ham, beef, beer, balsamic vinegar

Risotto asks that you hurry up and wait. Be patient, it says. But it'll punish you for pokiness. You've got to be quick on your feet. Like many Americans, I learned how to prepare it, if indirectly, from Italian culinary legend and cookbook author Marcella Hazan, who died from emphysema at age eighty-nine and was said to have smoked Pall Mall 100s and drank bourbon from start to finish every day. I like to use her risotto technique on other grains, too, like oats. This particular "oatotto" is a spin-off of a risotto with green apples that comes from the Alto Adige region and was one of the first I ever made. I've taken it totally out of Italy, replacing its white wine with ale and its Parmigiano-Reggiano with aged Gouda.

OATOTTO
WITH APPLES

serves 4

3 to 4 cups chicken or
vegetable stock

4 tablespoons (½ stick)
unsalted butter

2 tablespoons extra-virgin
olive oil

1 large red onion, finely chopped

2 apples, peeled, cored,
quartered, and thinly sliced
(I like Granny Smith)

1 cup steel-cut oats

1 cup beer (see Cooking Note)

¾ cup finely grated aged Gouda,
plus more for serving

¼ cup plus 2 tablespoons finely
chopped fresh chives

½ teaspoon salt, plus more
to taste

¼ teaspoon freshly ground black
pepper, plus more to taste

Bring the stock to a simmer in a medium saucepan over high heat. Reduce the heat to low to maintain the simmer as you continue cooking.

Melt 2 tablespoons of the butter with the olive oil in a large sauté pan over medium heat. Add the onion and cook until soft and translucent, about 5 minutes. Add the apples and oats and continue to cook, stirring often, until the oats emit a nutty aroma, 2 to 3 minutes. Add the beer and simmer, adjusting the heat as needed, until the liquid has evaporated, 8 to 10 minutes.

Add 1 cup of the simmering stock to the oats and cook, letting the grains soak up most of the liquid. Add another ½ cup stock, letting it absorb as before. Repeat this process until the oats have expanded and become chewy and slightly tender and a thick sauce has formed; this should take about 25 minutes total.

Turn off the heat and stir in the remaining 2 tablespoons butter, the Gouda, and ¼ cup of the chives. Season with the salt and pepper, tasting and adjusting as needed.

Divide the oatotto among 4 bowls and garnish each with some of the remaining 2 tablespoons chives. Serve with extra grated aged Gouda on the side.

COOKING NOTE Here, you want to use a malty brew that picks up on the flavors of aged Gouda—notably, an amber ale, light- to medium-brown ale, or brown porter. I plan on making this with hard cider someday soon.

Whenever I'm away from my kitchen too long, I start to get antsy. What I miss most of all is having my hands in a bowl of flour tossed with cold cubes of butter, pressing my fingers into the chilled fat and working it into the fluffy white powder. This is the first step for piecrust, biscuits, and, the dark horse of the pastry basket, scones. To make these softly crumbling oat-stippled wedges, I like to toast my grains, which draws out their nuttiness, just like it does for, well, nuts.

APPLE-OAT SCONES

makes 8 large scones

1 cup old-fashioned rolled oats

1¼ cups cold heavy cream

2 tablespoons plus 1 teaspoon maple syrup

3 cups all-purpose flour, plus more for dusting

1 tablespoon baking powder

1 teaspoon salt

12 tablespoons (1½ sticks) unsalted butter, cut into ½-inch cubes and chilled

1 cup chopped apple (I like Granny Smith)

1 tablespoon finely chopped fresh sage

1½ cups loosely packed grated aged Gouda

Preheat the oven to 375°F and place a rack in the center. Line a baking sheet with parchment paper.

Spread out the oats evenly on the prepared baking sheet and toast until lightly browned and fragrant, 7 to 9 minutes. Transfer to a small bowl to cool. Leave the oven on and line the baking sheet with clean parchment paper.

In a small bowl, whisk together the cream and maple syrup. In a large bowl, whisk together the flour, toasted oats, baking powder, and salt.

Add the chilled butter to the dry ingredients and, with your fingers, toss the cubes to coat. Break the butter up and rub it into the ingredients until it resembles a coarse meal.

Add the sweetened cream to the dry ingredients and, using a fork, incorporate just until the dough comes together. Add the apple pieces and the sage, and, with your hands, gently knead the dough in the bowl to integrate the mix-ins and smooth it out. Be sure any remaining dry ingredients stuck to the bottom

of the bowl have been worked in and the liquid is thoroughly incorporated. The dough should be wet and sticky. Quickly knead ¾ cup of the Gouda into the dough just enough to distribute it evenly.

Turn the dough out onto a lightly floured work surface and pat it into a 1½-inch-thick 7 x 7 inch square. Using a bench scraper, slice it into four 3½-inch squares, then cut each square on the diagonal, forming 2 triangles. Sprinkle the triangles with the remaining ¾ cup Gouda, patting the cheese onto the scones so it forms a small mound and sticks to the dough. This dough can be prepared and portioned in advance, layered between wax paper in an airtight container, and stored in the fridge overnight or the freezer for up to a month. Top the scones with Gouda before baking.

Transfer the scones to the prepared baking sheet and bake until they're golden brown and cooked through, 25 to 30 minutes. Let sit on the baking sheet for 10 minutes before transferring to a wire rack to finish cooling.

When the term *savory granola* began appearing on menus, I wrote it off as another example of chefs trying to convince us a garnish is news. With so many healthy-hippy and kitchen-sink hipster blends out there, it already seemed like anything could pass for granola. It was unavoidable: I was forced to try it and had to admit I liked it. Then I made it myself. My version of not-sweet granola was constructed for a not-sweet apple salad. Sprinkle leftovers on other salads, roasted vegetables, soups, plain yogurt, or fresh ricotta with a drizzle of honey. Prediction: After you're done mocking it, you're going to want to eat it all the time.

APPLE SALAD
WITH SAVORY GRANOLA

serves 4

SAVORY GRANOLA
(MAKES ABOUT 2¼ CUPS)

1 cup old-fashioned rolled oats

½ cup roughly chopped hazelnuts

¼ cup raw sesame seeds

2 teaspoons finely chopped fresh rosemary

1½ teaspoons caraway seeds

1½ teaspoons fennel seeds

¾ teaspoon flake salt

1 large egg white, lightly beaten

2 tablespoons extra-virgin olive oil

1½ teaspoons honey

SALAD

2 apples, cored, quartered, and thinly sliced (I like Granny Smith)

3 stalks celery, trimmed and sliced about ⅛ inch thick

2 tablespoons extra-virgin olive oil

1 tablespoon apple cider vinegar

1 teaspoon honey

1 teaspoon Dijon mustard

1 teaspoon curry powder

¼ teaspoon salt

Freshly ground black pepper to taste

¼ pound aged Gouda

Preheat the oven to 350°F. Line a baking sheet with parchment paper.

Make the granola. In a medium bowl, toss together the oats, hazelnuts, sesame seeds, rosemary, caraway and fennel seeds, and flake salt. Add the beaten egg white and stir to coat. Add the olive oil and honey and stir again to incorporate. Spread the mixture evenly on the prepared baking sheet. Bake until golden and toasty, stirring once halfway through, about 17 minutes. Let cool completely. The granola can be stored in an airtight container at room temperature for up to 2 weeks.

Make the salad. In a large serving bowl, toss together the apples and celery.

In a small bowl, whisk together the olive oil, vinegar, honey, mustard, and curry powder with a fork. Season with the salt and a few grinds of black pepper, whisking again to incorporate. Pour the dressing over the apples and celery and toss to coat.

Add ¾ cup granola and toss to distribute evenly. Just before serving, shave the Gouda over the salad using a cheese slicer or vegetable peeler.

SUBSTITUTION NOTE Try using fennel or broccoli—raw or roasted—in place of the celery. Yum.

BREAD
+
TOMATO
+
RICOTTA

We are rarely at a loss for bread or uses for it. Since the advent of canning, tomatoes have also been on call full-time. Once cooked, with their savoriness out in full force, they highlight the loaves' yeastiness. Soft, fresh, milky ricotta brings understated luxury to its commonplace companions.

	CHARACTER	SUBSTITUTE	TIP	COMPLEMENTS
BREAD	Sour, meaty, filling	Pasta, rice, beans	To accelerate staling, leave slices out for 24 hours, or cube and toast them at 350°F.	Herbs, butter, olive oil, garlic, olives, cheese, anchovies
TOMATO	Acidic, sweet, umami	Sweet bell peppers, sun-dried tomatoes, tomato paste, umeboshi paste, tamarind concentrate	Grating ripe, whole tomatoes with a box grater is a shortcut for pureeing them.	Herbs, chili peppers, sweet bell peppers, eggplant, garlic, olives, pasta, cheese, anchovies, bacon
RICOTTA	Creamy, mild, smooth	Cottage cheese, paneer, fresh goat cheese, queso fresco, silken tofu	Seek out the best-quality, freshest ricotta. It should be good enough to eat straight up.	Herbs, dried red chili flakes, dark leafy greens, balsamic vinegar, honey, olive oil, nuts, anchovies

One of the most romantic things you can do is offer someone a bowl of *pappa al pomodoro*. It can accurately be described as either a tomato-based bread dish or a bread-based tomato dish. Some like to think of (and eat) it as a soup. But the Italian word *pappa* translates to "porridge," and I happen to prefer the denser preparations. The more memorable ones have a toasted flavor that comes from browning the stale bread before adding the other ingredients, instead of throwing it in at the end. Mine starts with the bread and makes it the focal point of flavor and texture; any richer or denser and this wouldn't be pappa. When the weather turns cold, cook it for someone you love, with ricotta on top.

PAPPA AL POMODORO

serves 4

10 ounces rustic loaf, cut into 1-inch cubes (5 to 6 cups)

1 (14-ounce) can whole peeled tomatoes with their juices

¼ cup extra-virgin olive oil, plus more for finishing

4 tablespoons (½ stick) unsalted butter

6 large fresh sage leaves, thinly sliced into ribbons

4 medium cloves garlic, peeled and lightly crushed

1 teaspoon tomato paste

1¼ cups vegetable stock

½ teaspoon salt

¼ teaspoon freshly ground black pepper, plus more to taste

Sugar to taste (optional; see Cooking Note)

½ cup best-quality fresh ricotta cheese

Preheat the oven to 275°F.

Arrange the bread on a baking sheet in a single layer and bake until it has dried out and crisped up, tossing it once or twice along the way, 40 to 45 minutes.

Meanwhile, pass the tomatoes through a food mill set over a medium bowl and grind them to a pulp. Discard the remains.

When the bread cubes are ready, combine the olive oil and butter in a medium Dutch oven over medium-high heat. When the butter is melted and combined with the oil, add the bread. Using a wooden spoon, stir the cubes continuously until they begin to brown, 4 to 5 minutes. Add the sage and garlic, and continue to cook, still stirring, until the bread is golden, about 2 minutes more. Add the tomato paste and keep stirring for 1 minute to cook it through. At this point, the bread should be toasty brown.

Add the vegetable stock and cook until the bread absorbs it, 4 to 5 minutes. When the pan is nearly dry, reduce the heat to low and add the pureed tomatoes. Use a wooden spoon to gently break up the bread and incorporate it into the liquid. Cook until the bread has absorbed as much of the tomatoes' juices as possible and any remaining liquid has reduced, 8 to 10 minutes. You should have a thick porridge-like stew; the bread should be completely incorporated. Use your spoon to break down any remaining noticeably large chunks of bread.

Discard the garlic cloves and remove the pot from the stove. Taste the pappa and add the salt, pepper, and a pinch or two of sugar, if necessary. Serve immediately, dividing the pappa among 4 bowls. Top each with 2 tablespoons fresh ricotta, a liberal drizzle of olive oil, and some pepper.

COOKING NOTE Unripe and canned tomatoes are often too tart or, worse, have a metallic taste. Just a pinch or two of sugar will bring them around. I think it makes a big, positive difference.

Many moons ago, my friend Becca invited me to her annual Easter brunch and introduced me to her strata. Layered with tomatoes and fresh herbs, salty with prosciutto, and laden with what seemed like an Italianish pimiento cheese, the savory bread pudding was a crowning achievement. It was also lots of work, although I had a feeling it didn't need to be. A streamlined strata—one that requires less effort and fewer, but well-chosen, ingredients—is a better strata. With contributions from pimentón and harissa, this one is smoky and spicy and needs to sit in the fridge for at least 8 hours before baking. I'll be eating it every Easter now that Becca's moved away. She left her recipe behind, but I don't need it. (Sorry, Becca.)

SMOKY STRATA

serves 6

3 tablespoons unsalted butter

1 large onion, finely chopped (about 2¼ cups)

2¼ teaspoons salt

¼ teaspoon freshly ground black pepper

1 teaspoon smoked paprika

1 (28-ounce) can diced tomatoes, drained

⅓ cup plus 1½ tablespoons roughly chopped fresh oregano leaves

⅛ teaspoon sugar (optional; see Cooking Note, page 101)

1 day-old baguette (8 to 9 ounces), cut into 1-inch cubes (about 8 cups)

2 cups fresh ricotta cheese (1 pound)

1 cup finely grated Parmesan cheese

2¾ cups whole milk

9 large eggs

2½ tablespoons harissa

Melt the butter in a large heavy-bottomed skillet over medium heat. Add the onion and cook, stirring, until soft, 4 to 5 minutes. Add ½ teaspoon of the salt, the pepper, and the smoked paprika, and cook, stirring, for 1 minute to incorporate the seasoning. Remove the pan from the heat and stir in the diced tomatoes, ⅓ cup of the oregano, and another ½ teaspoon of the salt. Taste and add the sugar, if desired.

Arrange one-third of the bread cubes evenly in a 13 × 9-inch gratin dish or baking dish. Add one-third of the tomato-onion mixture around the bread cubes, scattering it evenly, followed by one-third of the ricotta, dolloping a few spoonfuls in the gaps and using the back of your spoon to smear it around. It doesn't have to be perfect or tidy. Sprinkle one-third of the Parmesan cheese on top. Repeat the layering twice more, reserving the final third of the Parmesan.

In a large bowl, whisk together the milk, eggs, harissa, and the remaining 1¼ teaspoons salt. Pour the mixture evenly over the strata. Cover the strata with plastic wrap and transfer it to the refrigerator so the bread can absorb the custard, at least 8 hours or overnight.

Preheat the oven to 350°F and place a rack in the center position. Remove the strata from the refrigerator and let it sit at room temperature for 30 minutes.

Just before putting it in the oven, sprinkle the top of the strata with the remaining 1½ tablespoons oregano and the reserved final third of Parmesan. Bake until puffed, golden brown, and cooked through, 45 to 55 minutes. Let stand for 5 minutes before serving.

Think about it: some of the most widely adored foodstuffs are just simple pairings of bread with tomato or cheese, or a combination of the three. In late summer when tomatoes are at the ripest, we slice the heirloom fruit and sandwich it between pieces of nothing-special white bread, with or without mayo. We love an old-fashioned grilled cheese, and some of us like to have it with a bowl of tomato soup. Then there's pizza—is anything more perfect? You don't need to do much to the ingredients, but I realized that if you treat each with a little extra care before putting them together, you get something equally simple but notably better. That's all I did here.

RICOTTA & TOMATOES
ON TOAST

serves 4

ROASTED TOMATOES

1 teaspoon sugar

½ teaspoon sea salt

½ teaspoon ground cardamom

¼ teaspoon freshly ground black pepper

1 pound cherry tomatoes, halved

3 tablespoons extra-virgin olive oil, plus more for greasing

RICOTTA

2 cups fresh ricotta cheese (1 pound)

4 tablespoons extra-virgin olive oil

3 teaspoons fresh thyme leaves

⅝ teaspoon fennel seeds

½ teaspoon flake salt

¼ teaspoon freshly ground black pepper

TOAST

4 (½-inch-thick) large slices crusty country loaf

1 clove garlic, halved

Extra-virgin olive oil, to finish

Flake salt

Honey (optional)

Preheat the oven to 375°F, placing one rack in the center position and another under the broiler. Lightly grease a medium roasting pan.

Roast the tomatoes. In a small bowl, stir together the sugar, sea salt, cardamom, and pepper. Arrange the tomatoes in the prepared roasting pan, cut-side up, in a single layer. Drizzle with 3 tablespoons olive oil and sprinkle with the sugar-spice mixture. Roast until bubbling and beginning to brown at the edges, 35 to 40 minutes. Remove the pan from the oven and increase the temperature to 400°F. Transfer the roasted tomatoes to a small serving bowl.

Prepare the ricotta. In a large bowl, season the cheese with 3 tablespoons of the olive oil, 2 teaspoons of the thyme, ½ teaspoon of the fennel seeds, the flake salt, and pepper. Use a rubber spatula to combine. Transfer to an 8-inch gratin dish. Use your fingertips to spread the cheese so it fills the dish, leaving slight dimples over the surface of the ricotta. Sprinkle the cheese with the remaining teaspoon thyme and ⅛ teaspoon fennel seeds, then drizzle with the remaining tablespoon olive oil. Bake until the top is golden brown, about 30 minutes. Remove it from the oven and heat the broiler.

Make the toast. Arrange the bread slices on a baking sheet. Toast the bread on both sides under the broiler, turning it over after the top just begins to brown, 2 to 4 minutes total. Remove the toast from the oven and rub the top of each with the cut side of one of the garlic halves and drizzle with olive oil.

To serve, slice each piece of toast in two, crosswise, and stack the halves on a plate. Set the plate, the just-baked ricotta, the bowl with the tomatoes, and a dish each of flake salt and honey (if desired) on the table. Diners should spread the cheese on the toast, top with the tomatoes, then garnish with a sprinkling of the flake salt and a drizzle of the optional honey.

BREAD

+

CHOCOLATE

+

OLIVE OIL

Using bread in desserts spares you the effort of making dough and helps you achieve an outcome that isn't cloying. Really good chocolate and olive oil share an inherent earthy fruitiness, and neither is too sweet. Bake with all three and you'll never fail to get something modern and grown-up.

	CHARACTER	SUBSTITUTE	TIP	COMPLEMENTS
BREAD	Yeasty, doughy, absorbent	Pound cake, croissant	When baking with bread, choose one rich in flavor that isn't too salty or crusty.	Warm spices, butter, brown butter, brown sugar, caramel, fruit, custard, cream cheese, eggs, nuts
CHOCOLATE	Bittersweet, fermented, smooth	Carob, cocoa powder, cacao nibs	Do not refrigerate or freeze chocolate. Store it at room temperature and note its expiration date.	Coffee, caramel, vanilla, cinnamon, nutmeg, ginger, chili, sesame, coconut, nuts, peanut butter, berries, figs, orange
OLIVE OIL	Fruity, peppery, green	Nut oil, melted coconut oil, melted butter	When baking (or drizzling) with olive oil, use *olio nuovo* for more pronounced flavor.	Vinegar, citrus, butter, herbs, chili peppers, salads, vegetables, olives, pasta, potatoes, yogurt, labneh, mozzarella, ricotta, seafood

Chef Anne Rosenzweig's legendary buttery, chocolate-seeped brioche bread pudding was served with a brandied custard pour-on that even kids wanted to drink at her long-gone Arcadia restaurant in New York City. In re-creating it, I've removed the butter and the brioche, using olive oil and sourdough where those were. The oil makes another appearance, stepping in for the brandy in the sauce. You'll really want to taste its flavor throughout the dish, so find the best-quality bottle you can, a greener-hued, pungent one with fruity notes—ideally a newly pressed olio nuovo. And you'll need to soak the toasted bread overnight, so plan accordingly. Allegedly, Anne has tried my version of her custard and is stealing the recipe. (I wonder if she drank it!)

CHOCOLATE BREAD PUDDING

serves 6 to 8

BREAD PUDDING

8 (1-inch-thick) slices sourdough Pullman bread, crusts on, cut into 1-inch cubes

⅔ cup extra-virgin olive oil

6 ounces bittersweet chocolate, roughly chopped

1 cup sugar

9 large egg yolks

2¼ cups heavy cream

¾ cup whole milk

1 vanilla bean, split and scraped

¼ teaspoon ground cinnamon

⅛ teaspoon salt

OLIVE OIL–CUSTARD SAUCE

2 large egg yolks

⅓ cup sugar

⅓ cup whole milk

1 cup heavy cream

Pinch of salt

¼ cup best-quality extra-virgin olive oil, preferably olio nuovo

(recipe continues)

COOKING NOTES

- To rig a double boiler equivalent, fit a heatproof bowl securely into a saucepan that's been filled with enough water to approach but not touch the base of the inserted bowl. The bowl shouldn't come into contact with the water in the pan.

- If you don't own a baking vessel large enough to hold the one with the bread pudding, fill an ovenproof pan with water and place it on the bottom rack of the oven right before you put the pudding in on a rack above it.

Preheat the oven to 425°F.

Make the bread pudding. In a large bowl, toss the bread cubes in the olive oil to coat, and let sit for 15 minutes to absorb all the oil. Spread them evenly on a baking sheet and toast until golden on all sides, tossing halfway through, 12 to 14 minutes total.

Fill the bottom of a double boiler with water and bring it to a gentle simmer over medium-low heat (see Cooking Notes). Add the chocolate to the top pot and, using a rubber spatula, stir it a few times to smooth it out as it melts. When it's completely melted, turn off the heat.

Whisk together the sugar and yolks in a large bowl until the mixture resembles a bright yellow lemon curd. In a medium saucepan over medium heat, bring the cream and milk to a near boil (you should see small bubbles gathering around the rim of the pan); swirl the pan a few times during heating to prevent a skin from forming on the surface. Whisking constantly, stream the cream-milk mixture into the beaten sugar and eggs to incorporate and make a smooth custard. Strain through a sieve set over a large bowl and discard the solids.

Whisk the custard into the melted chocolate to combine. Scrape the vanilla bean seeds into the pot, reserving the pod. Add the cinnamon and salt, and whisk just to combine. Add the reserved pod.

Arrange the bread cubes evenly in a 13 × 9-inch baking dish. Add the chocolate custard, including the split vanilla bean pod, cover with plastic wrap, and weight it down with a smaller pan so the bread stays submerged. Transfer the weighted baking dish to the refrigerator and let it sit overnight to soak through.

The next day, preheat the oven to 325°F.

Take the bread pudding from the refrigerator and remove the weight and plastic wrap. Cover the baking dish with aluminum foil. Prick the surface of the foil a few times with a fork to allow steam to escape. Place the covered baking dish in a larger roasting pan and carefully pour hot water around the baking dish to fill the pan (see Cooking Notes). Bake the bread pudding until any of the chocolate custard that hasn't been absorbed by the bread is glossy and set and a tester inserted into the center comes out clean, about 1 hour 15 minutes.

Meanwhile, make the sauce. In a small bowl, whisk together the yolks and sugar until the mixture resembles a pale yellow lemon curd.

Bring the milk and cream to a near boil in a medium saucepan over medium heat, swirling it occasionally to prevent a skin from forming on the surface. Remove the pan from the heat.

Whisk half of the milk-cream mixture into the bowl with the yolks and sugar. Slowly whisk the combined cream-yolk mixture back into the saucepan with the remaining milk-cream mixture and cook over medium-low heat. Continue to whisk the sauce until the cream starts to thicken, being careful not to let it boil, 10 to 15 minutes. Remove the pan from the heat. Whisk in the salt and strain the mixture through a sieve set over a medium bowl and discard the solids. Slowly stream in the olive oil, whisking to incorporate it. Cover the bowl and transfer it to the refrigerator to chill for at least an hour. Quickly whisk the custard again before serving to reincorporate. The sauce can be prepared a day in advance.

Discard the vanilla bean pod from the bread pudding. Serve warm with the olive oil custard on the side.

Until recently, I'd never made semifreddo, but I'd eaten a good deal of it. "Semi frozen" is what its name means. The Italian confection is a cross between gelato and mousse, yet unlike either of those, it can be sliced! You get these cold slabs of creamy, feathery velvet. My version would be perfumed with olive oil; that was all I knew. I didn't realize how easy the rest would be: you combine hot sugar with egg yolks, fold that into whipped cream, then flavor it however you'd like. Dotted with crunchy hazelnuts, my near-frozen triumph is quite sweet on its own, but a slightly herbal dark-chocolate sauce and a sour, almost salty piece of toast mitigate the sugar. The grassy oil is the tie that binds.

SEMIFREDDO TARTINE
WITH CHOCOLATE SAUCE

serves 8

SEMIFREDDO

2 cups heavy cream

1 cup plus 3 tablespoons sugar

7 large egg yolks

½ cup extra-virgin olive oil

½ teaspoon vanilla extract

½ teaspoon salt

1½ cups hazelnuts, toasted and roughly chopped (see Substitution Note)

CHOCOLATE SAUCE

1 cup heavy cream

6 sprigs fresh rosemary

2 tablespoons light corn syrup

7 ounces bittersweet chocolate, roughly chopped (about 1¼ cups)

3 tablespoons extra-virgin olive oil

TOAST

4 tablespoons (½ stick) butter

⅓ cup extra-virgin olive oil

8 (½-inch-thick) slices sourdough Pullman bread, crusts on

Make the semifreddo. In the bowl of a stand mixer fitted with the whisk, whip the cream to stiff peaks, starting on low speed and increasing to medium-high once the cream has thickened a bit. Using a rubber spatula, ease the whipped cream into a large bowl. Transfer it to the refrigerator to stay cold while you work on the rest of the semifreddo.

Line a 9 × 5-inch loaf pan with plastic wrap, leaving a substantial overhang around the perimeter.

Combine the sugar with ¼ cup water in a small saucepan over medium heat, stirring to mix, and clip a candy or deep-fry thermometer to the side of the pan. Cook until the liquid reaches the hardball stage (247°F to 250°F). Remove the pan from the heat.

Meanwhile, beat the egg yolks in the bowl of a stand mixer fitted with the whisk, whipping them at medium speed until they thicken and become a very pale yellow.

Run the mixer on low speed as you carefully drizzle the hot hardball sugar into the egg yolks, pouring it against the side of the mixing bowl to prevent splattering. When all of the sugar syrup has been added, increase the speed to medium and continue to beat until the bowl is cool to the touch. Slowly stream in the olive oil to incorporate. Add the vanilla and beat just to combine.

Gently fold the yolk mixture into the chilled whipped cream. Add the salt and fold again just to incorporate. Fold in the hazelnuts to combine.

Carefully pour the mixture into the prepared loaf pan, using your spatula to guide and scrape the mixture out of the bowl. Smooth over the surface and cover it with the excess plastic wrap overhang. Transfer the pan to the freezer to chill until the semifreddo is firm, at least 8 hours or overnight; it will keep for up to 3 days in the freezer.

(recipe continues)

Meanwhile, make the sauce. Bring the cream to a simmer in a medium saucepan over medium heat. Add the rosemary sprigs, using a wooden spoon to gently press them into the bottom of the saucepan to extract their flavor. Remove the pot from the heat, cover it, and let the mixture cool and infuse for 30 minutes. Discard the rosemary sprigs.

Return the saucepan with the infused cream to the stove over medium-high heat. Add the corn syrup and bring the mixture to a boil. Remove the pot from the heat and let the mixture cool for a few minutes, until it drops below 190°F, testing it with a candy or deep-fry thermometer.

Place the chocolate in a medium bowl. Pour the hot cream over the chocolate and let it sit undisturbed for 5 minutes to melt the chocolate. Using a rubber spatula, gently stir to combine. Start with small circles; once you see the cream and chocolate incorporating evenly, expand the circles, continuing to stir until the sauce is smooth and thoroughly combined. Add the olive oil and stir to incorporate. If you aren't using it right away, transfer the mixture to a sealed container and refrigerate it for up to 2 days. Rewarm in a small saucepan over low heat before serving.

About 25 minutes before you plan to serve the semifreddo, make the toast. Preheat the oven to 350°F, placing a rack in the center position.

Melt the butter with the oil in a small saucepan over medium heat. Place the bread on a baking sheet and brush the tops with one-third of the olive oil–butter mixture. Toast until golden on both sides, flipping the bread halfway through and brushing the second sides with another third of the olive oil–butter mixture, about 18 minutes total. Remove the bread from the oven, brush the tops with the remaining olive oil–butter mixture, and let it sit a few minutes to soak it up.

Meanwhile, unmold the semifreddo from its loaf pan, unfolding the plastic wrap and using that overhang to lift it out of the pan, inverting it onto a plate. Let it sit for 5 minutes to soften slightly.

To assemble, place a piece of the toast, twice-brushed side up, on a plate. Cut a 1-inch slice of the semifreddo and set it on top of the toast. Spoon some warm sauce over it and serve.

SUBSTITUTION NOTE Try almonds (regular or smoked) or pistachios instead of hazelnuts.

In Spain, kids come home from school, reach for a piece of white bread and a chunk of chocolate, and have at it. Spanish American chef José Andrés gave that snack a toque-ish face-lift by drizzling the bread with fruity olive oil before adding the bittersweet stuff, then running it under the broiler and finishing it with sea salt. Here, that dessert has morphed into a sandwich. Don't freak out, but I applied the proven technique for making the best grilled cheese: swipe mayo on the outer sides of the bread to get a beautiful patina on the crust. For a variation—or five—spread almond butter, orange marmalade, a berry jam, mascarpone, or ricotta on the interior of the non-chocolate-topped slice of sourdough.

GRILLED CHOCOLATE
SANDWICHES

makes 4

½ cup mayonnaise

1 tablespoon packed light
  brown sugar

8 (½-inch-thick) slices
  sourdough bread

¼ cup extra-virgin olive oil,
  plus more for drizzling

4 ounces bittersweet chocolate
  baking disks (about ¾ cup)

Flake salt to finish

Combine the mayonnaise and brown sugar in a small bowl. Lay out the bread slices on a work surface and spread the tops with half of the sweetened mayonnaise, to coat. Flip them over and brush their other sides with the olive oil. Divide the chocolate among 4 slices of bread, drizzle with a bit more olive oil (about 1 teaspoon per slice), and sprinkle with a pinch of salt. Cover the 4 chocolate-topped slices of bread with the remaining slices, oil-side down.

Heat a large cast-iron skillet on the stove, gradually increasing the heat from low to medium-low. Place 2 of the sandwiches in the skillet and cook until the bottoms are golden brown, 3 to 4 minutes. Flip the sandwiches with a spatula and cook until the second sides are golden brown, about 3 minutes more. The chocolate should be completely melted. Transfer the finished sandwiches to a rack, wipe the pan clean, and cook the remaining 2 sandwiches in the same way.

Let the sandwiches cool for a couple of minutes before cutting them in half and serving hot.

SEAFOOD

SQUID
+
CORNMEAL
+
PEPPERS

The vegetal sweetness of both corn and bell peppers means these two delicious brightly-colored things go great together. Cornmeal packages that "corny" flavor in soft or crispy form. Its old pal shrimp might seem a shoo-in for this covey, but overlooked, shyly nutty calamari has comparable flavor and costs less.

	CHARACTER	SUBSTITUTE	TIP	COMPLEMENTS
SQUID (CALAMARI)	Mild, silky, firm	Octopus, cuttlefish, shrimp, mussels, extra-firm tofu	Sauté squid quickly or braise it; anything in between gives you rubber.	Garlic, tomatoes, olives, chilies, citrus, sherry, olive oil, pasta, rice, pine nuts, chickpeas, sausage
CORNMEAL	Sweet, grainy, versatile	Semolina, ground oats, ground tortilla chips, corn flour	Grits are coarse-ground cornmeal; polenta can be made from medium- or coarse-ground cornmeal.	Corn, tomatoes, chives, onions, buttermilk, seafood, bacon
PEPPERS	Sweet, cleansing, crisp	Beets, carrots, leeks, tomatoes, zucchini	Red is the sweetest; yellow, orange, brown, and purple aren't far behind. Green is bitter.	Butternut squash, onions, tomatoes, eggplant, zucchini, corn, jicama, raisins, chickpeas, hazelnuts, anchovies, tuna, bacon, steak

I knew I liked hoecakes the first time I ate one of the thin, crispy-rimmed disks; although made with cornmeal, they reminded me of potato pancakes. I fell *in love* with hoecakes when I started making extra-large ones that filled up an entire skillet; I realized you can think of them as edible plates to build one-dish meals around and on. I designed this pan-size example to be a crunchy crash pad for squid and sweet peppers. Traditionally, you'd prepare your hoecakes with lard. But for this recipe, I use coconut oil to accent the cashews and bananas tossed into the stir-fry, which gets splotched with a peanut-less peanut sauce that sends me red-eye-gravy vibes and is worth making from scratch.

HOECAKE
WITH STIR-FRIED SQUID & PEPPERS

serves 4

CASHEW SAUCE

½ cup smooth roasted cashew butter

2 tablespoons soy sauce

1½ teaspoons sambal or your preferred red chili paste

1 tablespoon packed dark brown sugar

Juice of 2 limes

¼ cup hot water

SQUID STIR-FRY

1 pound cleaned squid

3 whole scallions, thinly sliced, dark green parts (reserve white and light green parts)

4 tablespoons unrefined coconut oil

1 sweet bell pepper, cored, seeded, and sliced lengthwise into ¼-inch strips, then halved crosswise (about 1¼ cups)

½ teaspoon salt, plus more to taste

½ cup unsalted roasted cashews or unsalted raw cashew pieces, toasted

1 banana, halved lengthwise and sliced into half-moons (about ¾ cup)

Fresh lime wedges, for squeezing

Freshly ground black pepper to taste

Cilantro leaves to finish

HOECAKE BATTER

1¼ cups finely ground cornmeal

¾ teaspoon salt, plus more to taste

1 teaspoon freshly ground black pepper

3 tablespoons plus 2 teaspoons melted unrefined coconut oil

Reserved white and light green scallion slices

(recipe continues)

> **COOKING NOTE** Drizzle any leftover cashew sauce over roasted vegetables or grilled chicken or seafood, or toss it with cold noodles.

Make the cashew sauce. In a food processor or a blender, combine the cashew butter, soy sauce, sambal, brown sugar, and lime juice. Puree until all the ingredients are incorporated and form a smooth paste, scraping down the sides with a rubber spatula as needed. With the motor running, trickle in the hot water to thin the sauce to a pourable consistency. Serve at room temperature. The sauce can be made ahead and stored in a covered container in the fridge for up to 3 days.

Stir-fry the squid. Rinse the squid under cold running water, then lightly pat it dry with paper towels. Separate the tentacles from the tubes. Cut the tubes into ½-inch-wide rings and leave the tentacles whole. Pat the squid dry again, then place it in a medium bowl. Add the dark green scallion slices, toss to combine, and set aside.

Heat a 12-inch cast-iron skillet on the stove, gradually increasing the heat from low to medium-high. Add 2 tablespoons of the coconut oil. When the oil is shimmering, add half of the bell pepper, sprinkle with a pinch of salt, and sauté until slightly softened, 2 to 3 minutes, stirring once or twice. Add half of the squid, sprinkle with another pinch of salt, and sauté, tossing continuously, just until the squid is opaque and cooked through, 1 to 2 minutes. Transfer the mixture to a large bowl and return the skillet to the stove. Repeat with the remaining 2 tablespoons coconut oil, bell pepper slices, and squid, adding it to the same large bowl once cooked. Wipe the skillet clean.

Add the cashews and banana to the large bowl and stir to incorporate. Squeeze lime all over the mixture. Season with ½ teaspoon salt and some black pepper, tasting and adjusting as needed. Shower the mixture with an ample handful of cilantro leaves.

Make the hoecake. In a small saucepan, bring 1⅔ cups water to a boil over high heat. In a large bowl, combine the cornmeal, salt, and black pepper. Add 1 cup of the boiling water to the cornmeal and stir to combine. Continue stirring and slowly add 2 more tablespoons water, 1 tablespoon at a time. The batter should be thin enough to pour but also thick enough to spread with a spatula once it is in the skillet. If the batter is too thick to pour, add more boiling water as needed, 2 teaspoons at a time. Add 1 tablespoon plus 2 teaspoons of the coconut oil to the batter and stir to combine. Stir in the reserved white and light green scallion slices.

Place the cleaned skillet over medium-high heat. Add the remaining 2 tablespoons coconut oil. When the oil is shimmering, pour the batter into the pan. Quickly and evenly spread out the batter with a spatula, leaving some space between the batter and the edges of the skillet. As the hoecake cooks, gently jiggle the pan occasionally to prevent sticking. As the edges begin to solidify, gently slide your spatula under the hoecake and begin to loosen it from the skillet. Cook until the edges are crisp and nicely browned and the rest of the hoecake is set, 8 to 10 minutes. Be sure it's completely loosened from the base of the skillet, then flip the hoecake with a spatula. Cook until the second side is ⅔ golden brown, 6 to 8 minutes more; the interior of the cake should be soft. Flip the hoecake out onto a large serving plate and sprinkle it with a pinch of salt.

Pile the warm sautéed squid and pepper mixture on top of the hoecake and spoon as much of the cashew sauce over it as you'd like. If you want, scatter a few more fresh cilantro leaves on top for garnish.

You've heard of shrimp and grits, but *this* is squid and polenta—I pulled a double switcheroo on the legendary Low Country duo. Plated with a jumble of peppers, this dish is closer to the shores of the Mediterranean than those of South Carolina. The vegetable side is a childhood relic my mom has been making since the mid-eighties, adapted with assists from paprika and tomato paste. You would be satisfied with any one of the three components here, but the best way to enjoy this is to drag the creamy polenta through the peppers' crimson-stained olive-oily gravy. I prefer the sweet bells at room temperature, so I let them cool while I prepare the seafood and cornmeal, or start a few days early and refrigerate them.

SAUCY PEPPERS, POLENTA & BOILED SQUID

serves 4

PEPPERS

½ cup extra-virgin olive oil

6 sweet bell peppers, cored, seeded, and cut into ½-inch dice

12 cloves garlic, halved lengthwise

2 shallots, thinly sliced

2 tablespoons tomato paste

2 tablespoons balsamic vinegar

1 tablespoon sugar

2 teaspoons Hungarian paprika

2 teaspoons salt, plus more to taste

Freshly ground black pepper to taste

16 fresh basil leaves

POLENTA

1 cup polenta (not instant)

1 tablespoon unsalted butter

1 teaspoon salt, plus more to taste

1 tablespoon extra-virgin olive oil

5¾ ounces feta, crumbled (about 1⅓ cups)

¼ teaspoon freshly ground black pepper, plus more to taste

SQUID

1½ pounds cleaned squid

⅓ cup pitted kalamata or niçoise olives, halved lengthwise

2 stalks celery, cut crosswise into ¼-inch-thick slices

1 cup loosely packed fresh flat-leaf parsley leaves

2 tablespoons fresh lemon juice

3 tablespoons extra-virgin olive oil

1 teaspoon fine sea salt

¼ teaspoon freshly ground black pepper

Dried red chili flakes to taste

Prepare the peppers. Heat the olive oil in a large skillet over medium heat. When the oil is shimmering, add the bell peppers, garlic, and shallots, and sauté until the peppers are softened and steam begins to rise, about 10 minutes. Stir in the tomato paste and cook until it's heated through, 3 to 5 minutes. Add the vinegar and sugar, stirring to incorporate. Stir in the paprika, followed by the salt and pepper, tasting and adjusting the seasoning as needed. Cook, stirring occasionally, until the peppers shrink and their liquid cooks out, 10 to 15 minutes. Add the basil leaves and bring the mixture to a simmer, reducing the heat as needed to prevent boiling. Continue cooking until the flavors have concentrated and you're left with a reddish-brown sauce, 8 to 10 minutes. Remove the pan from the heat and let cool. Stored in a sealed container in the refrigerator, the peppers will keep for up to 5 days; bring to room temperature before serving.

Make the polenta. In a medium saucepan over medium heat, combine the polenta with 4 cups water, the butter, and a generous pinch of salt. Bring to a simmer and cook until it begins to thicken, about 10 minutes, then reduce the heat to low and cover. Continue cooking for 1 hour, whisking periodically and being sure to scrape the bottom of the pan.

Meanwhile, cook the squid. Rinse the squid under cold running water, then lightly pat it dry with paper towels. Separate the tentacles from the tubes. Cut the tubes into ⅓-inch-wide rings and halve any larger tentacles lengthwise.

Prepare a large bowl of ice water. Bring 4 quarts water to a boil in a large pot over high heat. When it's boiling, salt it as you would for pasta. Add the squid and cook until just opaque, 40 to 60 seconds. Drain and immediately transfer the squid to the ice bath to stop cooking. Drain the squid again and pat dry with paper towels, then transfer it to a large bowl. Add the olives, celery, and parsley, and toss to combine. Add the lemon juice, olive oil, fine sea salt, pepper, and a pinch or two of chili flakes, and toss again to incorporate.

When the polenta is soft and no longer tastes gritty, remove the pan from the heat. Whisk in the olive oil. Stir in the feta. Season with the salt and pepper, tasting and adding more as needed.

To serve, spoon some polenta on 4 plates, followed by a bit of the peppers with their sauce, and top with the squid.

One of the most effective strategies for getting youngsters—and old fogeys—to eat an unfamiliar food is to fry it. Tasting something new has never scared me, but for a long time, I was terrified of deep-frying. Forced to take the plunge, I realized I enjoy the activity immensely. I encourage you to find your hot-oil bliss here and offer you a couple of enticements: curry powder–seasoned cornmeal for coating and munificently spiced chutney for dipping. The latter's ginger, mustard seeds, coriander, and turmeric are among the ground spices in a jar of curry seasoning. When you pop the crispy calamari tentacles, dabbed with the sweet-and-tangy condiment, into your mouth, it becomes a mosh pit for those flavors as they expand and collide.

CORNMEAL-CRUSTED CALAMARI
WITH RED PEPPER CHUTNEY

serves 4

RED PEPPER CHUTNEY

2 tablespoons neutral oil

1 (1¼-inch) piece fresh ginger, peeled and grated

½ teaspoon black mustard seeds

½ teaspoon ground coriander

½ teaspoon ground turmeric

½ pound ripe cherry tomatoes, quartered

½ pound red bell peppers (2 medium), cored, seeded, and cut into ½-inch dice (about 1¼ cups)

3 tablespoons packed light brown sugar

1 teaspoon salt

3 tablespoons fresh lemon juice

CALAMARI

2 quarts peanut oil

1 pound cleaned squid

1 cup all-purpose flour

1 cup finely ground cornmeal

2 teaspoons kosher salt, plus more for finishing

1 tablespoon curry powder

1 teaspoon freshly ground black pepper

Handful of fresh cilantro leaves, for garnish

Lime wedges, for serving

Make the chutney. Heat the oil in a medium saucepan over medium heat. When the oil is shimmering, add the ginger, mustard seeds, coriander, and turmeric, swirling to distribute. Fry the spices in the oil for 20 seconds, then add the tomatoes, bell peppers, sugar, and salt, stirring once to incorporate. Cook until the mixture takes on a jam-like consistency, stirring occasionally, 18 to 20 minutes. Stir in the lemon juice. Remove the pan from the heat and let the chutney cool slightly. It will keep, refrigerated in an airtight container, for up to 1 week.

Prepare the squid. Place the oil in a large, deep, heavy-bottomed pot over medium heat until a deep-fry thermometer registers 350°F to 375°F.

Meanwhile, rinse the squid under cold running water, then lightly pat it dry with paper towels. Separate the tentacles from the tubes. Cut the tubes into ½-inch-wide rings and halve any larger tentacles lengthwise.

Combine the flour, cornmeal, kosher salt, curry powder, and black pepper in a medium bowl.

Carefully and quickly fry the cilantro in small batches: drop a few leaves into the pot of oil just until crispy, about 10 seconds, using a spider or small strainer to remove and transfer them to a paper-towel-lined plate to drain.

Bring the oil back up to temperature, increasing the heat as needed to accelerate the process.

Meanwhile, add half of the squid to the flour mixture and toss to coat evenly, shaking off any excess back into the bowl. Using a spider or strainer, gently lower the coated squid into the hot oil, separating the pieces, and fry until golden and crispy, 2 to 3½ minutes. Remove and transfer the squid to a paper-towel-lined plate to drain. Season generously with kosher salt. Repeat with the remaining calamari, allowing the oil to return to temperature between batches.

Serve the fried squid immediately, on a large plate, in a serving bowl, or in a napkin-lined basket, garnished with the fried cilantro leaves and accompanied by lime wedges. Place the red-pepper chutney in a small bowl for dipping or spoon it over the squid.

CRABMEAT
+
MEYER LEMON
+
NORI

Delicately flavored, precooked fresh crabmeat is something of a treat. It should be spritzed with an equally elegant citrus such as floral Meyer lemons. Pressed and dried like papyrus, toasted nori is umami in paper form. Best known for encasing sushi rolls, the seaweed enhances any dish it's added to.

	CHARACTER	SUBSTITUTE	TIP	COMPLEMENTS
CRABMEAT	Subtle, sweet, flaky	Lobster, crayfish, shrimp	Refrigerated fresh lump crab is best, and most fishmongers stock it, but canned will do.	Herbs, asparagus, avocado, scallion, grapefruit, passionfruit, coconut, ginger, capers, chilies, butter, bacon
MEYER LEMON	Floral, acidic, thin skinned	Other types of lemon, lemon plus orange, yuzu	When Meyers aren't available, try regular lemons, but use less—they're larger and sharper.	Herbs, asparagus, dark leafy greens, vanilla, caramel, pasta, mascarpone, goat cheese, pistachios, almonds, hazelnuts, seafood
NORI	Briny, smoky, crisp	Korean roasted seaweek (i.e., *kankoku nori* in Japanese or *kim* in Korean)	Blend it into sauces and salad dressings, or use it as a garnish to jack up flavor.	Salads, soups, rice, pasta, seafood

Crab cakes are best when they're loosely contained, on the brink of falling apart in the pan but still holding it together. If you chill your patties before you fry them, they'll adhere without your having to bind them with bread crumbs or, what some people use, saltines. When I bust out the crackers, it's not for filler, and I go for broke with Ritz (the buttery-tasting best!). I whir them with nori (packed with seaside flavor!) to give my patties a goth crust (it's "whoa, cool, that's gnarly" dark).

CRAB CAKES
WITH TARTAR SAUCE

serves 4

- ½ cup mayonnaise (your preferred brand)
- 2 tablespoons small-diced bread-and-butter pickles or sweet gherkins
- 1 tablespoon small-diced shallot
- 5 sushi-size sheets (8 × 7 inches) toasted nori, torn into tiny pieces
- 2 Meyer lemons
- ¾ teaspoon salt, plus more to taste
- ¾ teaspoon freshly ground black pepper
- 1 pound fresh lump crabmeat
- 1 large egg, lightly beaten
- 1 tablespoon chopped fresh tarragon
- 2 tablespoons all-purpose flour
- 1 sleeve Ritz crackers (30 crackers)
- 2 tablespoons neutral oil
- 4 tablespoons (½ stick) unsalted butter

Make the tartar sauce. Combine the mayonnaise, pickles, shallot, 1 nori sheet, juice of 1 Meyer lemon, ¼ teaspoon of the salt, and ¼ teaspoon of the pepper in a food processor, and pulse together several times until the pickles are finely chopped and all the ingredients are well mixed but not pureed. Chill the sauce at least 1 hour before serving, or store it, refrigerated in a sealed container, for up to 5 days.

Make the crab cakes. Add the crab, egg, tarragon, zest of 1 Meyer lemon, the remaining ½ teaspoon salt and ½ teaspoon pepper, and the flour to a medium bowl. Using a rubber spatula, gently fold to combine. Cover with plastic wrap, and place in the freezer for 5 minutes to firm up. Line a large plate with plastic wrap. Form the crab mixture into 4 mounds and place them on the prepared plate. Cover the crab cakes with more plastic wrap and refrigerate for about 30 minutes or up to 1 day, or freeze for 15 minutes.

Add the remaining 4 nori sheets and the Ritz crackers to a food processor and pulse together into fine crumbs. Transfer the crumb mixture to a shallow bowl.

Heat a 12-inch cast-iron skillet on the stove, gradually increasing the heat from low to medium. Add the oil and butter and swirl to combine. Quickly and gently, one at a time, place each crab cake in the Ritz-nori mixture and pile the coating onto the patty with your hands. When the butter has melted and is no longer foaming, add the crab cakes to the pan and increase the heat to medium-high. Cook until browned on the bottom, about 5 minutes. Using a spatula, turn the cakes and brown their other sides, 3 to 4 minutes more.

Meanwhile, quarter the remaining Meyer lemon.

Season the crab cakes with salt as needed. Serve them hot with the quartered lemon wedges and tartar sauce alongside.

This winsomely crabby pasta is what you should serve someone you want to impress without looking as if you're trying too hard. I'd recommend it to wooers—and eleventh-hour cooks as well. Delicately flavored and soothingly filling, it's the paradigm of NBD cuisine. "What, this? Just something I whipped up on the fly," you'll say, shrugging, when your guests look at you worshipfully. They might also start adding nori to their pasta at home because of it. I like using the large sheets; they yield longer strips that pair well with the noodles. Cut them with kitchen scissors.

SPAGHETTI
WITH CRAB, LEMON & NORI

serves 4

Salt to taste

1 pound dried spaghetti

2 teaspoons pink peppercorns

3 Meyer lemons

¼ cup extra-virgin olive oil

2 tablespoons (¼ stick) unsalted butter

1 teaspoon fine sea salt, plus more to taste

1 cup fresh lump crabmeat

¼ cup finely chopped fresh chives

6 sushi-size sheets (8 × 7 inches) toasted nori, cut horizontally into ½-inch-wide strips

Bring 3 quarts water to a boil in a large pot over high heat. When the water is boiling, salt it. Add the spaghetti, stirring a few times right after you put it in the pot and then again, a minute later, to prevent sticking. Cook the pasta until al dente. Reserve ½ cup of the pasta cooking water, then drain the spaghetti.

Meanwhile, place the peppercorns in a mortar and grind them with a pestle. In a separate large pot, combine the zest of 2 Meyer lemons, the juice of all 3 Meyer lemons, the olive oil, and butter, and place over medium-low heat. Cook until the butter melts, whisking continuously to emulsify, about 3 minutes. Remove the pot from the heat, add ½ teaspoon of the fine sea salt and the mashed peppercorns, and whisk again to incorporate.

Add the cooked pasta to the pot with the lemon mixture and toss well to combine. Add the reserved pasta cooking water, 1 tablespoon at a time, as needed, until the sauce coats the spaghetti. Toss in the crabmeat, followed by the chives and the remaining ½ teaspoon fine sea salt, tasting and adding more if necessary. Add the nori strips, tossing again, separating any that stick together. The nori will wilt as you stir it through the pasta. Serve immediately.

If you make a sushi hand roll with actual crab instead of imitation crab, would it be an imitation, imitation crab roll? Sometimes, even the silliest questions lead to new recipes. That bit of wordplay sent me straight to my kitchen to figure out what this fake cone-shaped *tekka maki* with real seafood could be. Three batches of crab salad later, I had my answer. Dressing the shellfish with ingredients you don't find at sushi counters—like yogurt, dill, and harpoon-sharp French mustard—and rolling it in nori is a delicious way to psych someone out (and a crafty way to serve salad). It's a hand roll without rice, which I suppose means it's imitation sushi, if it can be called "sushi" at all.

CRAB SALAD HAND ROLLS

serves 4

12 scallions

2½ tablespoons extra-virgin olive oil

½ cup plain Greek yogurt

Zest of 1 Meyer lemon

2 teaspoons best-quality Dijon mustard

1 pound fresh lump crabmeat

1 stalk celery, finely chopped

1 tablespoon chopped fresh dill

½ teaspoon salt, plus more to taste

Freshly ground black pepper to taste

8 sushi-size sheets (8 × 7 inches) toasted nori, halved lengthwise

Heat a large cast-iron skillet on the stove, gradually increasing the heat from low to high. Place the scallions in a small bowl, drizzle them with ½ tablespoon of the olive oil, and toss to coat. Add the scallions to the pan in a single layer. Cook until charred on the first side, 4 to 5 minutes, then using tongs, flip and repeat on the other side. Remove the scallions to a plate to cool slightly, then slice them into ¼-inch pieces, trimming and discarding the roots.

Meanwhile, in a large bowl, whisk together the yogurt, lemon zest, mustard, and the remaining 2 tablespoons olive oil. Add the crabmeat and, using a spatula, fold to incorporate. Add the scallions, celery, and dill, and fold again to incorporate. Season with the salt and pepper, tasting and adjusting as needed.

Place one of the halved sheets of nori on a work surface with a longer side facing you. Put 2 tablespoons of the crab mixture on the left side, patting it down to fill about half the length of the sheet. Roll the nori from left to right to form a cigar shape, or diagonally from the lower left corner to the right to form a cone. Serve immediately.

SHRIMP
+
TOMATO
+
ALMOND

Some of the most dynamic ingredients are sweet with savory under-tones, or, like these three, the inverse: each is decidedly savory with a sweet streak. Shrimp's is brackish, tomato's tart, and almond's fruity and green. Because they contribute different kinds of sweetness, their collaborations are balanced and nuanced.

	CHARACTER	SUBSTITUTE	TIP	COMPLEMENTS
SHRIMP	Briny, sweet, firm	Lobster, crayfish, crab, squid, scallop	Don't knock frozen shrimp. Thaw in a bowl under cold running water before using.	Herbs, asparagus, artichokes, green peas, corn, citrus, garlic, coconut, white wine, capers, pasta, rice, beans
TOMATO	Sour, sweet, juicy	Grapes (for grape or cherry tomatoes); canned diced tomatoes (for chopped fresh tomatoes)	Cherry tomatoes are available year-round and are usually sweeter than off-season regular tomatoes.	Balsamic vinegar, fish sauce, lemon, saffron, ginger, sesame, capers, butter, miso, rice, seafood
ALMOND	Mild, sweet, crunchy	Pistachio, peanut, cashew, macadamia nut	Replace up to 20 percent of flour in batters with ground almond meal for an improved flavor.	Zucchini, bell peppers, cauliflower, fruit, coconut, ginger, sesame, caramel, chocolate, oats, rice, seafood, chicken, lamb

You'd find this salad in the picnic basket of my dreams, but my reality of living in a concrete jungle doesn't leave much room for leisurely repasts in the great outdoors. Fortunately, it tastes just as good at my desk as it would on a blanket in the grass. It's a lighter, herby take on shrimp salad: A buttermilk dressing full of bright-green chives updates the mayo-heavy base of old, while fresh parsley and tarragon tumble with the seafood. Tomatoes provide juicy surges of acid, salty-smooth Marcona almonds bring the crunch, and fried garlic chips keep you coming back. When fresh corn or peaches are in season, you should add them to the bowl— either or both.

SHRIMP & TOMATO SALAD

serves 4

1 pound medium to large shrimp, shelled and deveined

Salt to taste

Freshly ground black pepper to taste

3 tablespoons extra-virgin olive oil

5 cloves garlic, sliced as thinly as possible

18 ounces cherry or grape tomatoes (1½ pints), halved

¼ cup Buttermilk Dressing (recipe follows or store-bought), plus more as needed

1 tablespoon roughly chopped fresh flat-leaf parsley

1 tablespoon roughly chopped fresh tarragon

⅓ cup toasted salted Marcona almonds

Bring 3 quarts water to a boil in a large pot over high heat. Salt the water as you would for pasta. Add the shrimp and cook until it just turns pink and opaque, about 1 minute. Drain and let cool completely, about 15 minutes. Transfer to a large serving bowl and season with a pinch each of salt and pepper.

Heat the olive oil and garlic slices together in a large skillet over medium-low heat. When the garlic slices begin to bubble, after about 3 minutes, turn them over by stirring them. As soon as they begin to turn golden brown, 5 to 10 minutes, use a slotted spoon to transfer them to a paper-towel-lined plate to drain briefly. Add to the bowl with the shrimp and toss to combine.

Add the tomatoes to the bowl, season with salt and pepper, and toss to combine. Add ¼ cup buttermilk dressing, stirring to distribute it evenly. Add more, 1 tablespoon at a time, as desired. Add the parsley, tarragon, and Marcona almonds, and toss again to incorporate. Taste and adjust the seasoning as needed.

BUTTERMILK DRESSING

Makes about ¾ cup

¼ cup buttermilk

¼ cup plus 2 tablespoons mayonnaise

1 tablespoon fresh lemon juice

2 teaspoons Dijon mustard

¼ teaspoon Worcestershire sauce

2 to 3 tablespoons chopped fresh chives

¼ teaspoon salt

½ teaspoon paprika

In a medium bowl, whisk together the buttermilk, mayonnaise, lemon juice, mustard, and Worcestershire sauce to combine. Add 2 tablespoons chives, using up to a tablespoon more depending on your preference. Whisk to incorporate. Add the salt and paprika, and whisk again to incorporate.

Store in a sealed container in the refrigerator for up to 5 days.

In a small square adjacent to the fish market in Catania, a city on Sicily's east coast, there's a restaurant called Osteria Antica Marina that serves *busiate alla trapanese* with shrimp. I can still see the shallow bowl as it was placed down in front of me—and I can almost taste it. The pasta—tightly wound boing-boing-style corkscrews—coated in a tomato-and-almond pesto from its namesake town of Trapani is a specialty of the island. The freshly caught shellfish was a circumstantially appropriate touch, and one I knew I would replicate when I re-created the dish at home.

PASTA
WITH SICILIAN-STYLE PESTO & SHRIMP

serves 4

3 medium ripe tomatoes, halved

½ teaspoon fine sea salt, plus more to taste

¾ cup slivered blanched almonds, toasted

2 cloves garlic, roughly chopped

½ cup fresh basil leaves, torn into pieces

⅛ cup (6 or 7 medium to large) fresh mint leaves, torn into pieces

½ teaspoon freshly ground black pepper

½ teaspoon lemon zest

About 7 tablespoons extra-virgin olive oil

1 pound medium shrimp, shelled and deveined

8 ounces dried busiate (see Cooking Note)

4 tablespoons bread crumbs

Fresh lemon juice to taste, for serving

Preheat the broiler with a rack positioned about 6 inches from the oven's heating element.

Place the tomatoes, cut-side down, on a baking sheet. Broil until their skins are blackened, 12 to 15 minutes, checking on them every few minutes; they may smoke some. Remove from the oven and let cool. When the tomatoes are cool enough to handle, pinch off and discard their skins. Seed the tomatoes and finely chop them. Sprinkle with ½ teaspoon salt and put them in a fine-mesh sieve placed over a medium bowl, gently tossing them with your hands. Leave the tomatoes to drain as much as possible, up to 20 minutes.

Meanwhile, place the almonds in a food processor and pulse to a fine but grainy thick paste. Add the garlic, basil, mint, pepper, and lemon zest, and pulse to form a vibrant green paste. With the motor running, stream in up to 4 tablespoons of the olive oil to emulsify the pesto, creating a sauce. Err on the less-is-more side, so you don't wind up with an oily pesto or mask the flavors of the herbs and almonds. Transfer to a medium bowl (see How to Pesto, opposite).

Heat a large cast-iron skillet on the stove, gradually increasing the heat from low to medium-high. Add 2 tablespoons of the olive oil, increase the heat to high, and add the shrimp. Sauté them quickly, tossing continuously, just until pink and opaque, 2½ to 3 minutes. Transfer the shrimp to a plate and season with a generous pinch of salt.

Bring a large pot of water (about 3 quarts) to a boil over high heat. When the water is boiling, salt it. Add the busiate, stirring once right after you put it in the pot and then again, a minute later, to prevent sticking. Cook the busiate just until it's al dente. Reserve ⅓ cup of the pasta cooking water, then drain the busiate.

Meanwhile, wipe out the skillet from the shrimp and return it to the stove over medium heat. Add the remaining 1 tablespoon olive oil. When the oil is shimmering, add the bread crumbs and cook, stirring frequently, until brown and crispy, 2 to 3 minutes. Transfer to a small bowl.

Stir the drained tomatoes into the pesto base to combine. Taste and season with salt. Place a generous spoonful of the pesto in the bottom of a large serving bowl. Add the busiate to the bowl with the pesto. Add the shrimp and half of the remaining pesto, tossing so the sauce is evenly distributed and coats the seafood and pasta. If your sauce seems too thick, add some of the reserved pasta water to thin it (start with 1 or 2 tablespoons; add more as needed). If desired, continue to add more pesto by the spoonful, tossing it as you go. Top with the bread crumbs.

Squeeze some lemon juice on top and serve immediately.

> **COOKING NOTE** Busiate is a Sicilian pasta that's made using knitting needles—the noodles are twisted around them—and is optimal for holding a ragù or pesto. Another corkscrew shape like fusilli would do just as well.

HOW TO PESTO

Making pesto is an art, not a science. You're allowed to change it—to use less of one thing and increase the amount of another. Just make sure you taste it as you go, so you end up with something balanced. The key ingredients are herbs, nuts, cheese, garlic, and olive oil, but you should think of those in liberal terms and expand on them.

HERBS. The only stipulation is that these be fresh. You can easily retranslate herb as "leafy green thing" and branch out into the more flavorful salad greens like arugula (see page 165), spinach, dandelion greens, or even the tops of root vegetables like beets, carrots, or turnips. Blanched broccoli or broccoli rabe will also yield good results. So will green peas. Try combining these verdant options in whatever proportions you like as well.

NUTS. The pesto-crazed among us have extended our definition of nuts to include seeds—pumpkin, sunflower, and sesame are as welcome as almonds, pine nuts, pistachios, hazelnuts, walnuts, macadamias, chestnuts, cashews, pecans, and peanuts. Toasting any of these will intensify their flavor. Nuts are oily, and the softer ones are more so. If you use too many, you can get an oleaginous pesto, which is as unpleasant as it sounds. It's easily corrected: add more of the other ingredients and finish with less actual oil. Note that if you skip the nuts altogether, it'll still be pesto.

CHEESE. Parmesan is the pesto regular. I wouldn't include it in a seafood or fish dish, but you don't have to listen to me. Any hard grating cheese will work—Pecorino Romano, Grana Padano, (aged) Asiago, (aged) Manchego, Cotija, Swiss Gruyère, (aged) Gouda, or Cheddar. Blending is permitted.

GARLIC. Anyone who can't cope with garlic should just leave it out. It's been said that the allium should be the last thing added to your pesto; when it's overworked, it can get aggressively acerbic. I've found that blending it in at the last minute leaves me with huge, unprocessed pieces of garlic, which is way more offensive. So I add my garlic with the other herbs, and I try to process my pesto as quickly and minimally as possible.

OLIVE OIL. Does it have to be *olive*? No, but that's the standard, and it's used almost exclusively. As you get more experimental with the other ingredients, you may not appreciate this oil's assertive flavor. Sub in a neutral oil if that's your issue. Or try a complementary nut oil like almond, hazelnut, or walnut.

SEASONINGS. Lemon juice or zest brightens up pestos, and other types of citrus (or even vinegar) can do the same. Keep salt, ground pepper, and chili flakes on deck for the finishing touches.

Pesto can be applied to more than just your noodles. Spoon it onto roasted or grilled meats, poultry, and vegetables. Stir it into a bowl of beans, rice, or polenta. Swirl it into scrambled eggs, or top poached or fried eggs with it. Smear it onto sandwiches or, simpler still, toast. Whisk it into mayo for a hybrid condiment. Dress chicken salad with it.

To store, refrigerate your pesto in a sealed container for up to a week. You can freeze it for at least 6 months (in single-serving portions poured into an ice-cube tray placed in a resealable plastic bag) and up to a year (in a single sealed container). Just remember to wait before adding any cheese until you're ready to use the pesto and it has thawed.

I apologize for whatever unintentional rabble-rousing the following statement causes, but here goes: gazpacho is overrated. People are quick to say it's "so refreshing." Two bites in, I'm bored. But there's another, lesser-known Spanish soup that's also blended with leftover bread and served chilled, and it's underrated. *Ajo blanco* ("white garlic") is fortified with almonds, lots of them, and nary a vegetable in sight. It's typically garnished with plump grapes. This version comes with two surprises—plump grape tomatoes that have been candied to bring out their jammy fruitiness, and poached shrimp that lend texture and chew to the puree. You can serve the soup at room temperature or chilled. Conveniently, you can make all three components a day ahead and refrigerate them overnight.

ALMOND SOUP
WITH SHRIMP &
CANDIED TOMATOES

serves 4

½ cup sugar

Salt to taste

1 pound grape or cherry tomatoes (about 1½ pints)

1 dried bay leaf

½ teaspoon kosher salt, plus more as needed

12 medium to large shrimp, shelled and deveined

Freshly ground black pepper to taste

1½ cups plus 2 tablespoons ice water

1¼ cups slivered blanched almonds

3 medium cloves garlic, peeled

½ baguette, crusts removed, torn into pieces (2 cups)

¼ cup extra-virgin olive oil, plus more for drizzling

1 tablespoon plus 1 teaspoon red wine vinegar

½ teaspoon honey

In a large sauté pan, bring 1 cup water, the sugar, and a pinch of salt to a boil over medium-high heat, stirring occasionally. Add the tomatoes and the bay leaf. Reduce the heat to low and simmer gently, turning the tomatoes once or twice, until cooked through and soft, but not collapsing, 45 to 50 minutes. Using a slotted spoon, transfer the tomatoes to a medium bowl, leaving the liquid in the pan.

Increase the heat to high and reduce the liquid in the pan by half. It will be syrupy and thick. Pour the liquid over the tomatoes and let them cool. Discard the bay leaf.

Meanwhile, bring 3 quarts water to a boil in a large pot over high heat. Salt the water as you would for pasta. Add the shrimp and cook until they just turn pink and opaque, about 1 minute. Drain and let cool completely. Season with a pinch of salt and pepper. Split horizontally.

Combine 1 cup of the ice water, the almonds, garlic, and bread in a food processor or blender and let sit until the bread is softened, 4 to 5 minutes. Pulse into a smooth puree. With the motor running, add the remaining ½ cup plus 2 tablespoons ice water, the oil, vinegar, and honey, and process until the soup is emulsified—it should be creamy and silky. Add ½ teaspoon kosher salt and pulse just to incorporate. Taste and adjust the seasoning as needed.

Ladle the soup into 4 bowls. Garnish each bowl with 6 shrimp halves and 3 or 4 candied tomatoes. Finish with a drizzle of olive oil. If you'd rather serve the soup cold, after blending, refrigerate it in a sealed container for at least 3 hours or overnight; it will thicken up a bit.

> **COOKING NOTE** The tomatoes can be eaten warm, at room temperature, or even slightly chilled. Save extras for snacking, sandwiches, or cheese plates.

SALMON
+
PEAS
+
CELERY ROOT

A protein, a vegetable, a starch—it's a meal-planning formula as old as time, but one that welcomes strategic interpretation. Choose a starchy veg, like sweet green peas, and a vegetal starch, like celery root, also known as celeriac, though its ties to celery are just barely perceptible. Both benefit from and buffer salmon's flavorful fattiness.

	CHARACTER	SUBSTITUTE	TIP	COMPLEMENTS
SALMON	Oily, meaty, flaky	Arctic char, bluefish, striped bass	Splashing salmon in a solution of kosher salt and sake for 15 seconds removes fishiness.	Leek, scallion, ginger, lemongrass, asparagus, avocado, dark leafy greens, fennel, citrus, coconut, sesame, miso, pistachio
PEAS	Starchy, sweet, grassy	Carrots, spinach, sweet bell peppers, corn, adzuki beans, chickpeas, lentils	For most recipes, frozen peas are just as good as, if not better than, fresh.	Mushrooms, onions, sun-dried tomatoes, rice, pasta, heavy cream, eggs, ricotta, shellfish, halibut, veal, lamb, bacon, prosciutto
CELERY ROOT	Nutty, earthy, parsley	Parsnip, parsley root, potato, salsify, rutabaga, sunchoke	To peel the knobby vegetable, lop off the bottom and then slice off the skin in vertical strokes.	Parsley, mushrooms, horseradish, apples, chestnuts, mustard, walnuts, heavy cream, Gruyère, Parmesan, veal, bacon

I can't think of a time when I didn't love peas. But I do know the first truly great pea dish I ever ate: my mom's peas and prosciutto. Only later did I find out it's a traditional Roman preparation and not the modern novelty I'd imagined. I asked for the recipe so I could cook the cured pork–flecked peas and eat the whole batch myself in one sitting. I'd tell you to do the same, except those peas are intended as a side dish, not a complete meal. I've transformed the original so you can enjoy it for dinner without additional accompaniments. Instead of those nubs of prosciutto, you've got large tiles of spice-crusted salmon and casually smoky pieces of celery root.

ONE-PAN PEAS 'N' SALMON

serves 2

CELERY ROOT

2 teaspoons extra-virgin olive oil

1 cup (½-inch-diced) peeled celery root

¼ cup low-sodium chicken broth

1 small sprig fresh oregano

⅛ teaspoon salt

⅛ teaspoon smoked paprika

PEAS

2 tablespoons extra-virgin olive oil

2 cloves garlic, peeled

1 (10-ounce) package frozen peas, thawed

¼ teaspoon freshly ground black pepper

Salt to taste

SALMON

½ teaspoon flake salt, plus more to taste

1½ teaspoons celery seeds

1½ teaspoons cumin seeds

¼ teaspoon freshly ground black pepper

2 (6-ounce) skinless center-cut pieces of salmon fillet, each about 1¼ inches thick

1½ tablespoons extra-virgin olive oil

1 lemon, cut into wedges

Fresh oregano leaves

Make the celery root. Heat a large cast-iron skillet on the stove, gradually increasing the heat from low to medium. Add the olive oil. When it's shimmering, add the celery root, chicken broth, and oregano. Cook, stirring occasionally, until the celery root is beginning to soften and the broth has evaporated, 5 to 6 minutes. Season with salt and smoked paprika. Continue to cook, tossing frequently, until tender, using a spatula to scrape up and reincorporate any brown bits stuck to the skillet, 10 to 12 minutes more. Discard the oregano sprig and transfer the celery root to a small bowl.

Make the peas. Wipe out the skillet and return it to the stove over medium heat. Add the olive oil. When it's shimmering, add the garlic and cook, stirring until lightly browned, 3 to 4 minutes. Discard the garlic and return the prepared celery root to the pan, quickly tossing it a few times, then add the peas. Stir to combine, then add the pepper and stir again. Continue cooking until any residual water evaporates and the peas pick up some color and char slightly, 3 to 5 minutes. Reduce the heat to medium-low and cover. Cook for 5 minutes more to develop the flavors. Season with salt to taste. Transfer the peas and celery root to a serving platter or wide bowl, and cover with aluminum foil to keep warm.

Make the salmon. Using a mortar and pestle, crush together the flake salt, celery seeds, and cumin seeds, and transfer the mix to a shallow dish. Stir in the pepper to combine. Place the salmon, top down, on the spice mix, pressing the fish into the seasoning to coat.

Wipe out the skillet again and return it to the stove over high heat. Add the oil. When it is just smoking, add the salmon, one piece at a time, seasoned-side down. Cook until the crust is golden brown, 3 to 4 minutes. Flip the salmon, reduce the heat to medium, and sear until just cooked, 3 to 4 minutes more for medium-rare.

Transfer the salmon to a cutting board and let it rest for 5 minutes before slicing each piece into 1-inch tiles. Place the tiles on top of the peas and celery root. Squeeze lemon juice to taste over the salmon and scatter a few fresh oregano leaves on top. Finish with flake salt to taste.

This hands-off technique for roasting salmon ensures that the fish, no matter how thick, will always cook evenly and never emerge pathetically dry and flaky. The Green Pea Mash is my version of what the Brits call mushy peas. The celery root preparation is loosely—very loosely—based on the French dish *pommes Anna*, a crustless tart of the layered, thinly sliced tuber cooked in fantastically copious amounts of melted butter. This is not as orderly or comely, and celery root doesn't get crispy the way taters do; instead, it's got a homely aspect and a whole lot of roasted, buttery sweetness.

ROASTED SALMON
WITH CAST-IRON CELERY ROOT & GREEN PEA MASH

serves 4

SALMON

1 teaspoon olive oil

16 large fresh basil leaves

8 large fresh mint leaves

1 small shallot, finely sliced

Zest of 1 lemon

4 (6-ounce) thick skin-on salmon fillets

Kosher salt and freshly ground black pepper to taste

½ cup crème fraîche

1 tablespoon fresh lemon juice

1 tablespoon plus 1 teaspoon Dijon mustard

¼ teaspoon salt, plus more to taste

2 tablespoons finely chopped fresh chives

CELERY ROOT

2 small celery roots (1½ to 1¾ pounds), peeled and sliced ¼ inch thick

6 tablespoons (¾ stick) unsalted butter

½ teaspoon flake salt, plus more to taste

Freshly ground black pepper to taste

GREEN PEA MASH

2 (10-ounce) packages frozen peas, thawed

¼ cup roughly chopped fresh basil leaves

¼ cup roughly chopped fresh mint leaves

¼ cup extra-virgin olive oil

¼ cup plus 2 tablespoons crème fraîche

1¼ teaspoons salt, plus more to taste

¼ teaspoon freshly ground black pepper

Preheat the oven to 275°F.

Cook the salmon. Lightly grease a medium baking dish with ½ teaspoon of the olive oil. Make 4 small "patches" (that match the dimensions of the salmon fillets) of the herbs (2 basil leaves plus 1 mint leaf), a few shallot rings, and lemon zest. Place each piece of salmon on a patch, skin-side down. Rub the tops of the fillets with the remaining ½ teaspoon olive oil and lightly sprinkle each with kosher salt (about ⅛ teaspoon total) and pepper. Top each with another sprinkling of lemon zest and a few more shallot rings, then cover with the remaining basil and mint, as above. Roast the salmon until a fork inserted into the thickest part yields or an instant-read thermometer reaches 120°F for medium-rare, up to 35 minutes (see Cooking Note). Remove the salmon and let cool to room temperature. Discard all the herbs and shallot. Increase the oven temperature to 450°F.

COOKING NOTE The roasting time for the salmon will depend on its thickness. It can take up to 35 minutes, but thinner pieces may be done in 15 minutes. Check on the fish at 15 minutes and, if it needs more time, continue to check it every 5 to 10 minutes.

(recipe continues)

Meanwhile, make the celery root. Cut the celery root slices into pieces 1 to 1½ inches wide; don't worry if they're not uniform in shape. Melt 4 tablespoons of the butter in a small saucepan over medium heat.

Place a large cast-iron skillet on the stove over low heat for 5 minutes to warm. Remove it from the heat and add half of the melted butter, using a brush to spread it evenly over the bottom of the pan. Working quickly and starting in the center of the skillet, arrange enough of the celery root to fill the bottom of the pan in a single layer. It should look a bit like a messy puzzle with some cracks between the pieces. Brush the celery root layer with half of the remaining melted butter. Sprinkle with ¼ teaspoon of the flake salt and pepper to taste. Place the rest of the celery root on top of the others, creating a second layer. Brush the top with the remaining melted butter and sprinkle with the remaining ¼ teaspoon flake salt and pepper to taste.

Place the skillet over high heat. When you hear the butter begin to sizzle, after about 2 minutes, transfer the pan to the oven and bake until the vegetables have begun to brown around the edges, 20 to 25 minutes.

Meanwhile, melt the remaining 2 tablespoons butter in the small saucepan over medium heat. Remove the skillet from the oven and pour the melted butter over the celery root. Return the skillet to the oven and bake until the top layer of celery root is golden and the bottom layer's base has caramelized and turned a warm brown color, 8 to 10 minutes more. Transfer the celery root to a paper-towel-lined plate to drain any excess butter. Sprinkle with a pinch or two of flake salt.

While the celery root is in the oven, make the green pea mash. Bring ½ cup water to a boil in a large pot over high heat. Lightly salt it. Add the peas and boil for 2 minutes to cook through; drain. Transfer the peas to a food processor. Add the basil, mint, olive oil, crème fraîche, 1¼ teaspoons salt, and the pepper. Process together until a thick, slightly grainy puree forms. Taste and adjust for salt as needed.

Make the sauce for the salmon. In a small bowl, stir together the crème fraîche, lemon juice, Dijon mustard, and salt. Add the chives and stir again to incorporate. Season with salt to taste.

To serve, divide the salmon among 4 plates and top each fillet with a dollop of the sauce. Spoon some of the celery root and green pea mash alongside.

There was a time when tuna tartare was a strange, suspect dish—another menu stunt chichi restaurants pulled to alert the glam squad that *this* is where the action was. Soon it became a trend; now it's as common as a California roll or fish taco. And it's not just for tuna anymore; more flavorful and buttery, salmon is equally popular in this preparation. It's a breeze to make. I ignore the fancy garnishes and adulterate mine with popping green peas and pickled celery root. Quickly firming up the salmon in the freezer will make it easier to cut. While it's in there, you can ready the other ingredients. I can't resist stirring honey mustard into the dish and recommend you do the same, starting with a tablespoon.

SALMON TARTARE
WITH PEAS & PICKLED CELERY ROOT

serves 4

1 pound filleted skinless sushi-grade salmon

¾ cup thawed frozen peas

½ cup drained Pickled Celery Root (recipe follows)

1½ tablespoons fresh lemon juice

1 tablespoon chopped fresh dill

2 tablespoons chopped fresh chives

1 tablespoon neutral oil

¼ teaspoon flake salt, plus more to taste

¼ teaspoon freshly ground black pepper, plus more to taste

Lemon zest to taste

Honey mustard to taste (optional)

Thick-cut potato chips, pita chips, and/or toasted and olive oil–drizzled country bread, for serving

Place the salmon in the freezer for 20 minutes to firm up.

Meanwhile, in a small saucepan over medium heat, cook the peas just to warm through. Remove the pan from the heat and let the peas cool.

Transfer the salmon to a cutting board, cut it into ½-inch cubes, and place it in a large bowl. Add the cooled peas, pickled celery root, lemon juice, dill, chives, and oil. Stir to incorporate. Add the flake salt and pepper, sprinkle some lemon zest over the mixture, and stir to combine, tasting and adjusting the seasonings as needed. If you want, add honey mustard, starting with 1 tablespoon; if needed, add more to taste.

Transfer the tartare to a serving bowl and serve immediately with your choice of accompaniments.

PICKLED CELERY ROOT

Makes 1 cup

1 cup peeled and finely diced celery root

½ cup unseasoned rice vinegar

1½ tablespoons sugar

2 teaspoons kosher salt

3 thin strips lemon peel

Place the celery root in a medium bowl.

In a small saucepan, combine the vinegar, sugar, salt, lemon peel, and 1½ tablespoons water, and bring to a boil over medium-high heat, stirring to dissolve.

Pour the hot liquid over the celery root and use a smaller bowl or plate on top to submerge it. Let it cool to room temperature.

Remove the weight, cover the bowl with plastic wrap, and refrigerate for 1 hour. At this point, the pickles are ready. If you want to let their flavors deepen or are making them in advance, you can transfer them to a sealed container and refrigerate for up to 2 weeks.

POULTRY + MEAT

CHICKEN LEG

+ APPLE

+ SHALLOT

Gamey-tasting birds take kindly to fruit with well-proportioned measures of acid and sugar, and to the sharp sweetness of alliums. Dark chicken meat is at the lower end of the gamey spectrum, so a less acidic fruit—apple—and a moderately tame allium—shallot—flatter it.

	CHARACTER	SUBSTITUTE	TIP	COMPLEMENTS
CHICKEN LEG	Earthy, meaty, moist	Duck, goose, turkey leg	A chicken leg (aka leg quarter) comprises the drum and thigh of the bird.	Stone fruit, dried fruit, onions, cabbage, root vegetables, mushrooms, pumpkin, chestnuts, sausage, bacon, red wine
APPLE	Sweet, mild, juicy	Quince, stone fruit, figs, dried fruit	The peel of an apple is good for you. Remove it only for aesthetic or texture-related reasons.	Endive, fennel, cabbage, carrots, beets, turnips, potatoes, prunes, maple syrup, honey, chicken livers, game birds, pork
SHALLOT	Concentrated, mild, sweet	Yellow onion	For easier peeling, cover shallots with boiling water for 5 minutes before trimming their bases.	Balsamic vinegar, stone fruit, fish, duck, beef

In the Alsace region of France, there's a specialty called *baeckeoffe* ("baker oven"), a peasant stew of wine-marinated meats combined with vegetables, potatoes, herbs, and spices that's placed in an earthenware vessel, sealed with a flour-paste-like dough, and slow-cooked in the oven. When I tried it for the first time, it had been made with chicken and tasted like someone was giving me a snuggly bear hug. Meanwhile, in Central Asia, you'll find equally cosseting one-pot dinners of meat simmered with fruit. I drew on both specialties to devise a diversely spiced, heartwarming stew of my own. I like to serve it with toasted crusty bread and a fresh green salad. Note that the bird needs to marinate for at least 12 hours before heading to its pot.

A CHICKEN IN EVERY POT

serves 6

- 8 large shallots, chopped (about 2½ cups)
- 2 large carrots, peeled and chopped (about 1 cup)
- 2 cloves garlic, minced
- 1 teaspoon ground turmeric
- 1 teaspoon paprika
- 1 teaspoon whole juniper berries (see Cooking Note)
- ½ cinnamon stick
- 2 dried bay leaves
- 2½ teaspoons fine sea salt, plus more to taste
- ¾ teaspoon freshly ground black pepper, plus more to taste
- 3 tablespoons finely chopped fresh flat-leaf parsley, plus more for garnish
- 1 (750 ml) bottle dry white wine (I like Riesling)
- 6 chicken legs
- ⅓ cup extra-virgin olive oil
- 3 medium Yukon Gold potatoes, peeled and cut into 1-inch pieces (about 5 cups)
- 5 pounds apples, peeled and cut into 1-inch pieces (4 heaping cups)
- 1½ cups chicken stock

In a large bowl, combine the shallots, carrots, garlic, turmeric, paprika, juniper berries, cinnamon, bay leaves, salt, pepper, parsley, and white wine. Add the chicken, turning to coat. Cover with plastic wrap and refrigerate for 12 to 24 hours.

When you're ready to cook the chicken, preheat the oven to 350°F.

Strain the marinade, reserving it, and separate the chicken from the vegetables. Return the cinnamon stick and bay leaves to the marinade.

In a large Dutch oven, heat the oil over medium-high heat. Pat the chicken dry and, when the oil is shimmering, add the chicken and cook, flipping it halfway through, until brown on both sides, about 15 minutes total. Transfer the chicken to a plate. Add the vegetables from the marinade to the pot and sauté until they've taken on some color, 12 to 15 minutes.

Return the chicken to the pot, layering it with the potatoes and apples. Add the stock and 1 cup of the reserved marinade along with the bay leaves and cinnamon stick. Let the liquid come to a boil. Cover and transfer the pot to the oven. Roast the chicken until it's cooked through and tender, the apples are soft, and the potatoes are fork-tender, about 40 minutes.

Remove the pot from the oven. Stir the contents, incorporating the vegetables up from the bottom. Discard the bay leaves and cinnamon stick. Let cool for 10 minutes, then garnish with parsley. Taste and season with salt and pepper. Serve hot.

COOKING NOTE Avoid the juniper berries when serving and caution others against eating them. They lend incredible flavor but eaten whole taste bitter.

My mother had a fancy upbringing, complete with a revolving door of cooks. One was a woman named Christine, a soap-opera fanatic who excelled at desserts and always wore a nurse's cap. She served an especially memorable crispy Parmesan-and-bread-crumb-coated chicken. Sadly, her tenure ended when it was discovered she'd hidden a suitcase in a tree, containing items she'd stolen from the family. Years later, Mom found a similar poultry preparation in a vintage English cookbook and adapted it to make what we now call Christine's Chicken with roasted pears. This is my take on it. To start, you'll need to leave your seasoned chicken to sit overnight or longer.

CHRISTINE'S CHICKEN
WITH ROASTED APPLES + SHALLOTS

serves 4 to 6

CHICKEN

6 chicken legs

Fine sea salt to taste

¾ teaspoon freshly ground black pepper

1¼ cups grated Parmesan cheese

1½ cups bread crumbs

2 cloves garlic, crushed

2 tablespoons (2 ounces) chopped fresh flat-leaf parsley

1 cup (2 sticks) unsalted butter, melted

APPLES + SHALLOTS

1 cup packed dark brown sugar

6 whole cloves

3 apples, halved and cored (I like Honeycrisp)

⅜ teaspoon ground cinnamon

6 shallots, peeled

¼ teaspoon salt

2½ tablespoons unsalted butter, cut into ¼-inch cubes

Prep the chicken. When salting your bird, assume about ¾ teaspoon per pound. Season the chicken legs with fine sea salt and ¼ teaspoon of the pepper and let them rest in a covered container or zip-top bag in the refrigerator overnight or for up to 2 days.

The next day, preheat the oven to 350°F. Line a roasting pan and a baking sheet each with aluminum foil.

Prepare the apples and shallots. In a small saucepan, bring the brown sugar and ¾ cup water to a boil over medium-high heat. Cook for 5 minutes, until the sugar is melted and incorporated.

Stick one clove in each apple half. Sprinkle them with the cinnamon, then rub it in. Place the spiced apples and the shallots in the prepared roasting pan and sprinkle them with the salt. Pour the molten brown sugar over the apples and shallots. Dot the mixture with the butter. Set aside.

In a shallow bowl, combine the Parmesan, bread crumbs, remaining ½ teaspoon pepper, the garlic, and parsley.

Place the melted butter in a medium bowl. Pat the chicken dry. Dip each chicken leg in the butter to coat, then into the crumb mixture, turning to coat. Place the chicken, skin-side down, on the prepared baking sheet. Pat some of the remaining crumb mixture on top of any pieces that need it. Reserve the remaining melted butter and crumb mixture.

Place the apples and shallots and the chicken in the oven to roast. After 40 minutes, baste the chicken with the reserved melted butter every 20 minutes. When the top of the chicken is golden and crispy, after 50 to 60 minutes, turn each piece over and, careful not to burn your fingers, pat the additional crumb mixture on the skin side to coat it amply. Continue to roast the chicken until the skin side is deep golden brown and the meat is cooked through. Remove from the oven, tent with foil, and let it rest for 15 minutes.

At the same time, spoon the sugar liquid in the roasting pan over the fruit and shallots every 20 minutes until they're nicely caramelized and the fruit is knife tender, 80 to 90 minutes. Transfer the apples to a plate, leaving the shallots in the roasting pan. Return the pan to the oven, increase the temperature to 475°F, and continue to cook the shallots until they are well caramelized and syrupy, about 10 minutes. (The chicken will still be in the oven at this point and may finish cooking a few minutes before the shallots.) Remove the shallots from the oven. Transfer the apples back to the roasting pan, turning them to coat in the syrup.

Serve the apples and shallots with the chicken, spooning the syrup over the chicken and placing some of the fallen crumb mixture on the apples.

As a spoiled little girl, when I was introduced to tarte tatin—the upside-down, flaky-crusted French dessert with its burnished apples shining in their buttery burnt-sugar coating—I greedily demanded more, Veruca Salt–style. Learning you can tatin-ize other fruit (tomatoes, even!) set my heart aflutter. I once saw a recipe for the upside-down tart made with *shallots*. So why not caramelize them with the apples and make a meal of it? Confit the chicken (plus garlic) just as you would duck (that is, cook it slowly, in lots of fat), pile the shredded meat on the base, and cover it with puff pastry (store-bought is A-OK). Lucky you, there will be leftover caramelized garlic for spreading onto toast or stirring into mashed potatoes.

SAVORY APPLE TARTE TATIN

serves 4 as a main course
or 6 as an appetizer

2 chicken legs

Salt and freshly ground black pepper to taste

2 cups extra-virgin olive oil, plus more as needed

1 sprig fresh thyme, plus more leaves to taste

1 head of garlic, unpeeled, halved crosswise

3 fresh sage leaves, thinly sliced

1 tablespoon unsalted butter, plus more for greasing

3 apples, peeled, cored, quartered, and cut into ½-inch slices (4 cups; I like Pink Lady)

6 to 8 shallots, cut lengthwise into ½-inch-wide slices (2 cups)

1 tablespoon maple syrup

1½ tablespoons balsamic vinegar

1 sheet frozen puff pastry (about ½ pound), thawed (see Cooking Note)

All-purpose flour, for dusting

Flake salt to finish (optional)

Preheat the oven to 300°F.

Season the chicken with salt and pepper. Place the chicken in a medium Dutch oven and cover completely with the olive oil. Add the thyme sprig and garlic. Place over medium-high heat and cook just until bubbles start to form on the surface of the oil, about 3 minutes.

Transfer the pan to the oven. Cook until the meat can be easily pierced with a knife, about 2 hours. As it cooks, the oil should just barely bubble. Check it occasionally, adjusting the oven temperature as needed.

Let cool slightly, then strain the chicken, reserving the oil and caramelized garlic. Wrapped in plastic and placed in a sealed container, the meat can be refrigerated for up to 5 days. Stored in a sealed container, the reserved oil can be refrigerated for up to a week.

Increase the oven temperature to 400°F, placing a rack in the upper third.

Scrape the skin and any visible fat from the chicken legs and discard it. Remove all the meat from the bones and discard the bones. Roughly chop the meat and transfer it to a medium bowl. Add a few of the reserved caramelized garlic cloves, smashing them with a fork and incorporating them into the chicken (I use about 6). Taste and adjust for salt and pepper as needed. Add the sage and stir to combine.

Heat a large cast-iron skillet on the stove, gradually increasing the heat from low to medium. Add 2 tablespoons reserved confit oil and the butter. When the butter has melted and combined with the oil, sauté the apples, working in batches as needed, stirring occasionally, until lightly brown and slightly soft, about 12 minutes. Season with salt and pepper. Remove the apples from the pan.

Add another tablespoon of the reserved confit oil to the pan, then add the shallots. Reduce the heat to medium-low and sauté, stirring occasionally but carefully to leave them intact, until softened and beginning to caramelize, about 10 minutes. Season with salt and pepper, and transfer to a cutting board.

Generously grease a 9-inch round cake pan with butter. Drizzle the pan with the maple syrup and balsamic vinegar. Alternate the cooked apple slices and shallot slices in the pan, arranging them in tight concentric circles. Scatter thyme leaves over the surface, then top with the chicken. Drizzle 2 more tablespoons of the reserved confit oil over the chicken.

Remove the thawed pastry dough from the refrigerator and let it sit on a lightly floured surface for 5 minutes. Carefully unfold it, then, using a lightly floured rolling pin, roll out the puff pastry to a ⅛-inch thickness. Trim it so it's a little larger than the cake pan. Brush the excess flour off the dough, then place it over the pan, gently pressing it around the chicken as you tuck the edges of the pastry into the pan. Use a fork to prick the pastry all over.

Bake until the pastry is golden and crisp, about 30 minutes. Remove the tart from the oven and wait 5 minutes before setting a plate upside down on the top of the pan. Carefully invert the tart onto the plate and, if you'd like, finish with a sprinkling of flake salt. Slice and serve.

COOKING NOTE Defrost frozen puff pastry in the refrigerator overnight. My preferred store-bought brand is Dufour, but Pepperidge Farm is more widely available and always reliable. Alternatively, buy a sheet or two off your neighborhood bakery.

CHICKEN BREAST
+
MOZZARELLA
+
ARUGULA

Chicken breasts may seem depressingly straightforward, when really they're blank canvases ready to be transformed into something desirable. Mozzarella is the chicken breast of cheese. That means it's also capable of great change. Their shared neutrality makes them compatible with each other and with livelier personalities, like peppery arugula.

	CHARACTER	SUBSTITUTE	TIP	COMPLEMENTS
CHICKEN BREAST	Neutral, lean, succulent	Turkey breast, veal, pork loin, extra-firm tofu, eggplant, cauliflower, mushrooms	To defrost frozen chicken breasts, transfer them to the fridge for at least 5 hours.	Mustard, chutney, curry (paste or powder), alliums, nightshades, capers, white wine, Parmesan, goat cheese, prosciutto
MOZZARELLA	Milky, bland, highly meltable	Provolone, scamorza, burrata, stracciatella, halloumi, smoked mozzarella	Fresh is best, especially for raw applications, but processed low-moisture mozzarella is fine for melty toppings.	Balsamic, onions, mushrooms, nightshades, sun-dried tomatoes, olives, peaches, plums, bread, nuts, anchovies, sausage, veal
ARUGULA	Peppery, nutty, leafy	Dandelion greens, mustard greens, watercress, chicories, spinach, kale	Stir leaves through cool water to clean, then transfer them to a salad spinner or paper towels to dry.	Balsamic vinegar, lemon, Parmesan, ricotta, goat cheese, nuts, roasted or grilled pork, steak

Next time you visit your local sushi spot, order the *goma-ae*. It's a blanched vegetable appetizer named for its sesame dressing, which has a smidgeon of sweetness and tastes a little like—but better than—peanut sauce. Although spinach tends to be the bed for the topping, green beans sometimes provide a surface. Here I've gone and done it with arugula, and I've turned it into a chicken salad. You just want to wilt the leaves; overcooking them will result in some serious acridity, as opposed to the palatable bitterness that makes arugula my number one salad green.

CHICKEN SALAD GOMA-AE

serves 4

4 scallions, trimmed and cut into thirds

4 pounds skin-on, bone-in chicken breasts (2 or 3 whole breasts)

Boiling water

1½ pounds arugula leaves

1 pound fresh mozzarella, sliced into 1 × ½-inch strips

1 medium cucumber, peeled, halved lengthwise, seeded, and cut into ¼-inch thick half-moons

¼ cup soy sauce

2 tablespoons plus 2 teaspoons sugar

½ cup tahini

2 tablespoons plus 2 teaspoons white sesame seeds, toasted

½ teaspoon salt, plus more to taste

Fill a large, tight-lidded Dutch oven or heavy-bottomed pot two-thirds full with cold water. Add the scallions, cover, and bring to a rolling boil. Turn off the heat and add the chicken— it should be completely submerged by 2 inches. If there's not enough water in the pot, add more boiling water as needed. Cover the pot and let the chicken sit on the stove, with the heat off, until its flesh is white and its juices run clear, about 2 hours. If it's not quite done, cover the pot again and bring to a simmer, cooking the chicken for 10 minutes more. Transfer to a plate and let cool.

Meanwhile, bring a large pot of water to a boil and salt as you would for pasta. Prepare a large bowl of ice. Add a third of the arugula to the boiling water and blanch for 10 seconds. Using a slotted spoon, quickly transfer the arugula to a strainer, keeping the water in the pot boiling. Immediately plunge the strainer into the bowl of ice and run very cold water over the leaves to shock them. Keeping the arugula in the strainer, drain the leaves, transfer to paper

towels, and squeeze dry. Transfer the blanched arugula to a large bowl, using your fingers to separate it. Repeat twice with the remaining arugula.

When the chicken is cool enough to handle, remove and discard the bones, skin, and fat. Pat the meat dry with paper towels, then shred it into small bite-size pieces and add it to the bowl with the arugula. Toss to combine. Add the mozzarella and cucumber to the salad and toss again to incorporate all the ingredients.

Make the dressing. In a medium bowl, whisk together the soy sauce, sugar, and tahini. Slowly whisk in ¼ cup water to thin out the sauce. Add the toasted sesame seeds and whisk to incorporate.

Pour one-third of the dressing into the base of a large serving bowl. Add the salad and toss to incorporate. Continuing to toss, stream in another third of the dressing so the salad is evenly coated. Add more dressing as desired. Season with the salt. Serve at room temperature.

My brother John's "usual" is a grilled chicken sandwich from his local deli. I wanted to convince him he could cook a vastly improved, undemanding chicken dish himself, should he have a notion to try. An incredibly crisp-skinned, succulent piece of poultry was the goal; together we achieved it. It involves a buttermilk bath and hot-hot-hot cast-iron skillet that starts on the stove and moves to the oven. He likes his with roasted broccoli. I prefer mine with a simple salad of arugula, sun-dried tomatoes, mozzarella, and a vinaigrette made from the marinade used to flavor the cheese. When you get the notion, give yourself at least a 12-hour lead to marinate the chicken, and allot 4 hours for steeping the mozzarella.

CHICKEN PAILLARD & ARUGULA SALAD
WITH MARINATED MOZZARELLA

serves 4

CHICKEN

- 4 skin-on boneless chicken breast halves (10 to 12 ounces each; see Cooking Notes)
- 2 tablespoons extra-virgin olive oil
- 1 tablespoon lemon zest
- 1 tablespoon fresh lemon juice
- 1½ teaspoons freshly ground black pepper, plus more to taste
- 2 teaspoons kosher salt, plus more to taste
- 2 cups buttermilk
- Wondra or all-purpose flour, for dusting (see Cooking Notes)
- 6 tablespoons neutral oil

SALAD

- ½ cup plus 2 tablespoons extra-virgin olive oil, plus more as needed
- 1 large clove garlic, minced
- ¼ teaspoon dried red chili flakes
- 1 tablespoon finely chopped fresh oregano leaves
- 1 tablespoon finely chopped fresh basil leaves
- 1 teaspoon coarse sea salt
- ½ teaspoon freshly ground black pepper
- 8 ounces fresh water-packed *ciliegine* or *bocconcini* (see Cooking Notes), drained
- ½ cup dry sun-dried tomatoes
- 5 ounces wild or baby arugula
- 2 teaspoons fresh lemon juice

Prepare the chicken. Place the chicken between two pieces of plastic wrap and pound it until the breasts are about ½ inch thick. Place 2 chicken breasts each into two large resealable plastic bags.

Whisk together the olive oil, lemon zest and juice, black pepper, and kosher salt in a large bowl. Continuing to whisk, add the buttermilk. Evenly divide the marinade between the two bags. Seal each and refrigerate the chicken for 12 to 24 hours, turning a few times throughout.

Meanwhile, marinate the mozzarella for the salad. Heat 2 tablespoons olive oil in a small skillet over medium heat. When the oil is shimmering, add the garlic and chili flakes, stirring just until the garlic starts to color, about 2 minutes. Remove the pan from the heat and stir in the oregano, basil, ½ teaspoon of the sea salt, and ¼ teaspoon of the black pepper. Let sit for about 5 minutes to cool slightly.

Pack the mozzarella balls into a 16-ounce lidded glass jar or sealed plastic container. Pour the prepared oil over them. Add the remaining ½ cup olive oil to cover, using more if needed, seal the jar, and turn it a few times to coat the cheese. Refrigerate for at least 4 hours or overnight.

Before you are ready to cook the chicken, soak the sun-dried tomatoes in a small bowl filled with warm water until reconstituted, about 1 hour. Drain, then roughly chop them.

Preheat the oven to 400°F.

Remove the chicken breasts from the marinade and pat them dry with paper towels. Dust the skin-side of each breast with Wondra flour (about 1 tablespoon total), shaking off any excess, and set the chicken on a plate.

Heat a large cast-iron skillet on the stove, gradually increasing the heat from low to medium-high. Add 3 tablespoons of the neutral oil. When the oil is shimmering, add 2 chicken breasts, skin-side down. Cook, occasionally pressing with a spatula, until browned, 5 to 7 minutes.

Transfer the skillet to the oven, roasting the chicken until it's just cooked through and its juices run clear, 8 to 12 minutes. Remove the skillet from the oven and flip the breasts over. Sprinkle each with a pinch of kosher salt and black pepper. Let them sit in the skillet for 1 minute, then transfer to a plate and cover with foil. Repeat with the remaining 3 tablespoons neutral oil and chicken breasts.

Meanwhile, make the salad. In a large bowl, season the arugula with the remaining ½ teaspoon sea salt and ¼ teaspoon black pepper, tossing to incorporate. Add the sun-dried tomatoes and toss again to combine. Dress the salad with the lemon juice and 1 tablespoon plus 1 teaspoon of the flavored oil from the mozzarella, tossing to coat. Add about half of the mozzarella. Save the remaining cheese in its marinade for another use. Sealed in an airtight container, both will keep for up to a week in the fridge; bring to room temperature before serving.

To serve the salad and chicken separately, family-style, toss the arugula in a large serving bowl and place the chicken on a platter. To present it as one dish, place the chicken breasts on a large platter, then top or surround them with the salad. Alternatively, you can plate the meals individually.

COOKING NOTES

- Your butcher can debone the chicken. If you're doing it yourself, use a thin, flexible knife to cut the flesh away from the bones, being careful to leave the skin in place.

- *Ciliegine* are—as per their Italian name—"little cherry"–size balls of fresh mozzarella packed in water; the *bocconcini* ("little mouthfuls") are larger versions thereof. If your market doesn't have them, you can get a regular-size sphere of fresh mozzarella and roughly cut it into smaller pieces.

- What Kleenex is to tissue, Wondra is to instant flour. Finely ground and low protein, it's quick to dissolve and less prone to gumminess and clumping than regular flour. Since it's precooked, you don't have to worry about keeping it on the stove long enough to remove any raw flavor. I like to dust chicken or vegetables with it before frying or baking them; it yields the thinnest, crispest of coatings.

Something we never admit but all know is true: Even bad chicken Parmigiana is good. We totally eat—and love—it cold, same as pizza. It can be made with suck-o tomato sauce or questionable "cheese" that looks like baked Shrinky Dinks, and still we accept it. Imagine what properly melty mozzarella-blanketed chicken Parmigiana could be under the best circumstances—coated with potato chips, smeared with a bright electric-green sauce—and you should arrive at this tour de force. Try it in sub form on a long, thick roll, slapped with extra pesto, topped with arugula leaves, and hit with a squeeze of lemon. Or, bypass the broiler and eat the chicken without the cheese or pesto, enjoying the maximum crunch from the chips.

POTATO-CHIP CRUSTED CHICKEN
WITH ARUGULA PESTO

serves 4

1½ cups packed fresh arugula

½ cup packed fresh flat-leaf parsley leaves

1 medium clove garlic, roughly chopped

¼ cup plus 2 tablespoons toasted hazelnuts, roughly chopped

2 ounces Parmesan cheese, coarsely grated (scant ¾ cup)

¼ teaspoon kosher salt, plus more to taste

½ cup extra-virgin olive oil

¼ cup plus 1 tablespoon all-purpose flour

Freshly ground black pepper to taste

¼ cup whole milk

1½ cups finely crushed kettle-style potato chips

¾ teaspoon cayenne pepper

4 skinless, boneless chicken breast halves (8 to 10 ounces each)

8 (¼-inch-thick) slices fresh unsalted mozzarella

In a food processor, pulse together the arugula, parsley, garlic, hazelnuts, Parmesan, and salt to form a paste, scraping down the sides of the bowl as needed. Slowly stream in the olive oil as you continue pulsing to form a smooth, bright sauce. Taste and adjust for salt as needed. (See How to Pesto, page 139.)

Place a baking rack on a parchment-lined baking sheet and coat the rack with cooking spray. Set a rack in the oven so that when your chicken is raised on the baking rack, it's 2 or 3 inches away from the broiler. Preheat the oven to 400°F.

Spread ¼ cup flour on a large plate and season with a pinch each of salt and black pepper. Add the milk to a medium bowl and season with a pinch each of salt and black pepper. Fill a separate medium bowl with the potato chip crumbs, the remaining 1 tablespoon flour, and the cayenne. Stir to combine.

Season each chicken breast on both sides with a pinch each of salt and black pepper. One at a time, dip each breast in the seasoned flour to coat, shaking off any excess, then dunk in the milk, letting any excess drip off, and roll through the potato-chip mixture, pressing to coat. Place on the prepared baking rack. Pat any remaining potato-chip coating on top of the breasts.

Bake the chicken breasts until their crusts are golden, they're just cooked through, and their juices run clear, 18 to 20 minutes. Remove the chicken from the oven and turn on the broiler.

Cover each breast with 2 pieces of mozzarella. Return the chicken to the oven and broil until the cheese is bubbling and just beginning to brown, about 4 minutes. Transfer to a large serving platter and let rest for 5 minutes. Gently smear a few spoonfuls of the pesto over each breast and serve.

GROUND BEEF

+

EGGPLANT

+

PARSNIP

Ground beef is easily incorporated into potato-topped casseroles, formed into burgers served with fries, stuffed into vegetables like fleshy eggplant, or stir-fried with said same. A three-in-one would be perfectly predictable. Stet the aubergine and meat, swap the potato for sweeter parsnip, and it's still perfect, but without the predictability.

	CHARACTER	SUBSTITUTE	TIP	COMPLEMENTS
GROUND BEEF	Neutral, versatile, crumbly	Any other ground meat or poultry, ground tofu, loose sausage, chopped mushrooms	Optimal lean-to-fat burger ratio is 70/30. Beef marked "lean" will range from 73/27 to 96/4.	Alliums, tomatoes, mushrooms, spinach, potatoes, beef stock, red wine, chili peppers, raisins, pine nuts, cheese
EGGPLANT	Fleshy, meaty, dense	Bell peppers, mushrooms, extra-firm tofu	Salt eggplant *before* frying it; otherwise, doing so is optional (and possibly useless).	Tomatoes, onions, garlic, miso, vinegar, sesame, pine nuts, feta, goat cheese, yogurt, shrimp, lamb, pork
PARSNIP	Sweet, starchy, firm	Potato, salsify, carrot, rutabaga, turnip, parsley root, celery root, sunchoke	Shaved thin using a mandoline or peeler, it can be enjoyed raw in salads.	Apples, pears, sweet potato, winter squash, coconut, dates, chestnuts, hazelnuts, pistachios, walnuts, Parmesan, lamb, bacon

Some days for lunch, my grade-school cafeteria served shepherd's pie, with a stiff-crusted brick of mashed potatoes on top and a gravy-thick brown sludge of ground beef with frozen peas and carrots beneath. Those were not good days. And that was not proper shepherd's pie. In Britain, you can only call it by that name if it's made with lamb, and it can be quite good. Greece has a ground-lamb bake of its own: moussaka. It's a layering of fried eggplant, meat, and a crown of béchamel, and it can be great. I've engineered a Greco-Anglo fusion with ground beef and a parsnip topping you can make a day ahead. It's the best of both countries.

NYC SHEPHERD'S MOUSSAKA

serves 4 to 6

- 1 cup plus 1½ tablespoons extra-virgin olive oil
- 3 dried bay leaves
- 2 allspice berries
- 1 large yellow onion, finely chopped
- 1 pound ground beef
- 1 (14-ounce) can whole peeled tomatoes
- 2 tablespoons tomato paste
- ½ teaspoon ground cinnamon, plus more for dusting
- Pinch of ground cloves
- 1½ teaspoons red wine vinegar
- ½ teaspoon sugar
- 1 teaspoon kosher salt, plus more to taste
- ¼ teaspoon freshly ground black pepper
- 1 pound parsnips, peeled and sliced about ⅛ inch thick
- ½ cup heavy cream
- ½ cup whole milk
- 2 tablespoons (¼ stick) unsalted butter
- ¼ teaspoon ground nutmeg
- 1½ large eggplants (about 2¼ pounds total), sliced into ¼-inch-thick rounds
- 4 tablespoons grated Gruyère cheese
- 4 tablespoons grated Parmesan cheese

Make the meat sauce. Heat 1½ tablespoons of the oil in a large saucepan over medium-high heat. When the oil is shimmering, add the bay leaves, allspice, and onion. Cook until the onion is soft, about 5 minutes. Add the ground beef and continue to cook, stirring occasionally, until browned and all the liquid has evaporated, about 30 minutes.

Meanwhile, add the tomatoes and their juices to a medium bowl and, using your hands, break them down completely.

Add the tomato paste, ½ teaspoon cinnamon, and a pinch of ground cloves to the ground beef. Cook for 2 minutes to caramelize the paste and intensify the flavors. Add the vinegar, sugar, ½ teaspoon of the salt, half the crushed tomatoes (save the rest for another use), and 1 cup water. Bring to a boil, then reduce the heat to medium-low and partially cover the pan, cooking until almost all of the liquid has evaporated, about 1 hour 10 minutes. Remove the pan from the heat. Discard the bay leaves and allspice berries. Season with the pepper. Taste and adjust for salt as needed.

While the meat sauce is reducing, make the parsnip puree. Bring the parsnips, cream, milk, and butter to a boil in a medium saucepan over medium-high heat. Reduce the heat to low, cover, and gently simmer, stirring occasionally, until the parsnips are very soft, 20 to 25 minutes. Uncover and continue to cook until the liquid has reduced by half, about 5 minutes more. Stir in the remaining ½ teaspoon salt and the nutmeg. Transfer the mixture to a blender and puree until smooth, or use an immersion blender in the saucepan. Set aside to cool. This can be made a day ahead and refrigerated in a sealed container. Bring to room temperature before using.

(recipe continues)

COOKING NOTE To salt the eggplant, place the slices in a colander set on a plate or in the sink to catch any draining liquid and generously sprinkle with kosher salt (about 1 tablespoon plus 1 teaspoon total). Let the eggplant sit for 30 minutes. This will leach out excess liquid.

Preheat the oven to 350°F.

Salt the eggplant (see Cooking Note). Rinse the slices and pat them dry with paper towels. Dust with cinnamon.

Heat the remaining 1 cup oil in a large cast-iron skillet on the stove, gradually increasing the heat from low to medium-high. When the oil is shimmering, add the eggplant, and, working in batches as needed, fry the eggplant until golden brown, about 10 minutes, flipping it halfway through. Transfer the eggplant to paper towels to drain. Wipe out the skillet. Let the pan sit for a few minutes until it's cool enough to handle.

Spread half the parsnip puree in the bottom of the skillet and sprinkle 2 tablespoons each Gruyère and Parmesan over it. Spoon the meat sauce over the puree, spreading it to the edge in an even layer. Lay the eggplant on top, overlapping the slices to cover the surface. Spread the rest of the parsnip puree over the eggplant, and sprinkle the remaining cheese on top. Bake until the edges are browned and the cheese is melted, 30 minutes. Let cool for 15 minutes.

Use a sharp knife to cut each portion, loosening it from the edge of the pan, then, carefully, slide a spatula under the section to pull it out and gently transfer it to the plate so the soft moussaka retains its shape.

Sadly, for many home cooks, outdoor grilling and the charred burgers it enables are an impossible dream. But I had a thought: could you simulate that smoky, blackened experience with scorch-skinned eggplant? Anyone who has prepared baba ghanoush, the Levantine dip made from that vegetable, knows how to singe its purple skin over a burner (or under a broiler). I took my flame-darkened aubergine and mixed it into my ground beef. Then I buried cooling, salty feta in each patty. Derived from spicy Southeast Asian sambals, parsnip relish is an upgrade from ketchup; it can jazz up any burger, hot dog, or deli sandwich, and accompany meat or fish that has been grilled—or pan-seared or roasted. Because who needs a grill anyway?

EGGPLANT-BEEF BURGERS
WITH PARSNIP RELISH

makes 4

PARSNIP RELISH

3 medium parsnips (1 pound), peeled and grated

2 shallots, thinly sliced

2 cloves garlic, minced

2 teaspoons sea salt

½ cup sugar

1 teaspoon dried oregano

1½ teaspoons dried red chili flakes

¼ cup apple cider vinegar

Roughly chopped fresh flat-leaf parsley, for serving

BURGERS

1 small eggplant (9 to 10 ounces)

2 tablespoons extra-virgin olive oil

½ teaspoon smoked paprika

½ teaspoon kosher salt, plus more to taste

1 pound ground beef

2 ounces feta cheese, cut into 12 cubes

Freshly ground black pepper to taste

1 tablespoon unsalted butter

4 hamburger buns, toasted (I like Martin's)

Make the relish. In a large heavy-bottomed, nonreactive saucepan, combine the parsnips, shallots, garlic, sea salt, sugar, ½ cup water, the oregano, and chili flakes. Bring to a boil over high heat. Reduce the heat to medium-low and simmer, stirring occasionally, for 30 minutes. Add the vinegar and continue to cook until the parsnips are translucent and a bit spicy, about 30 minutes more; overall the relish should look like sauerkraut. Transfer the mixture to a small bowl to cool completely. Sealed in an airtight container, it can be stored in the refrigerator for up to 2 weeks. Before serving, stir in as much parsley as you like.

Preheat the oven to 375°F.

Make the burgers. Prick the eggplant all over with a fork and place it directly over the burner's flame on medium heat. Char the outside of the eggplant, using tongs to turn it until the entire surface is blackened evenly, about 15 minutes. (Alternatively, you can do this in the oven, under the broiler, on a baking sheet.) Transfer it to a baking sheet and roast in the oven until the flesh is mushy soft, 20 to 30 minutes. When the eggplant is cool enough to handle, trim it, remove and discard the skin, and place the flesh in a food processor. Add the olive oil, smoked paprika, and kosher salt, and process into a smooth puree. Let cool to room temperature and transfer to a large bowl.

Add the ground beef to the puree and stir just to incorporate. Divide the mixture into 8 small piles about 3 inches wide. Top one of the piles with 3 cubes of feta, then place another pile on top of it, gently pressing to form a thick patty and completely enclose the feta. Repeat to form 4 patties. Season on both sides with kosher salt and pepper.

Heat a large cast-iron skillet on the stove, gradually increasing the heat from low to medium. Add the butter. When the butter is melted and sizzling, increase the heat to high and add the patties. Cook without moving them until a crust forms on the bottoms, about 5 minutes. Flip the burgers over and cook to your liking, about 4 minutes more for medium-rare. Remove them from the skillet and let rest for 5 minutes.

Place the burgers on the toasted buns and top each with some of the parsnip relish.

When I returned from South Africa, the first thing my mother asked was if I'd eaten bobotie, a national specialty. The curried lamb casserole was brought to that country by Dutch settlers in the seventeenth century. When a livestock shortage hit, eggs were used to make up the meatless difference, and the dish's distinguishing custard cap was baked into place. Dried fruit and nuts were a contribution from the Malaysian population. I sub parsnips for the traditional carrots and apples, and ground beef for the lamb. A customary accompaniment, tomato *smoor* is a sweet and mildly hot condiment; when prepared with eggplant, it becomes more of a side dish.

PARSNIPPY BOBOTIE
WITH EGGPLANT SMOOR

serves 6 to 8

BOBOTIE

2 large eggs

1½ cups whole milk

1½ teaspoons fine sea salt, plus more to taste

2 slices stale white bread, crusts removed, torn into pieces

1 to 2 tablespoons neutral oil

2 small yellow onions, thinly sliced

1 or 2 cloves garlic, minced

1 to 2 tablespoons curry powder

1 teaspoon ground turmeric

¾ cup sliced almonds, toasted

2 large parsnips, peeled and grated (about 14 ounces total)

8 dried apricots, finely diced

⅓ cup firmly packed golden raisins (2 ounces)

2 tablespoons mango chutney, plus more for serving

½ teaspoon freshly ground black pepper, or more to taste

2 pounds ground beef

3 or 4 dried bay leaves

Cooked rice, for serving (optional)

SMOOR

¾ cup extra-virgin olive oil

2 medium eggplants (14 to 16 ounces each), cut into ½-inch dice

1¼ teaspoons fine sea salt, plus more as needed

1 large yellow onion, cut into ¼-inch slices

12 ounces cherry tomatoes, halved

1 jalapeño pepper, stemmed, seeded (optional), and minced

1 tablespoon sugar

Preheat the oven to 350°F.

Make the bobotie. In a small bowl, whisk together the eggs, 1¼ cups of the milk, and 2 pinches of salt to taste until smooth. Cover the custard base with plastic wrap and refrigerate until ready to use. Place the bread and the remaining ¼ cup milk in a separate small bowl and set aside.

In a large sauté pan, heat 1 tablespoon of the neutral oil over medium-low heat. When the oil is shimmering, add the onions and cook, stirring frequently, until just beginning to caramelize, about 20 minutes. If the onions start to scorch, add the remaining 1 tablespoon neutral oil. Add the garlic and cook until fragrant, about 1 minute. Add the curry powder and turmeric, and cook, stirring, until the onions are coated and aromatic, 30 to 60 seconds. Transfer the mixture to a large bowl, let cool slightly, then add the almonds, parsnips, apricots, raisins, chutney, and soaked bread along with any remaining milk. Season with 1½ teaspoons salt and ½ teaspoon pepper and stir to thoroughly incorporate.

Add the meat to the bowl and mix well. Transfer the mixture to a large round baking dish and pat it down evenly. Tuck the bay leaves into the dish, leaving them exposed to pull out after baking.

Bake the bobotie until it's just firming up, about 30 minutes. Carefully remove the dish from the oven and drain off any excess fat. Pour the custard base evenly over the top, return the dish to the oven, and bake until the custard is set, about 20 minutes more.

Meanwhile, make the smoor. In a large sauté pan, heat ½ cup plus 2 tablespoons of the olive oil over medium-high heat. When the oil is shimmering, add the eggplants and cook, stirring occasionally, until softened and golden, 11 to 15 minutes. Season with ½ teaspoon of salt, transfer to a medium bowl, and set aside.

Wipe out the pan and add the remaining 2 tablespoons olive oil over medium-high heat. When the oil is shimmering, add the onion and cook, stirring occasionally, until it begins to turn golden, 10 to 15 minutes. Reduce the heat to medium-low and continue to cook until the onion is browning on the edges, 10 to 15 minutes. Stir to prevent burning. Add the tomatoes, jalapeño, and sugar; stir well. Cook on low heat until warmed through, 10 to 15 minutes. Season with ½ teaspoon of salt and transfer to the bowl with the eggplant, stirring to combine. Add the remaining ¼ teaspoon salt and taste, adjusting the seasoning as needed.

Let the bobotie cool for about 10 minutes. Remove the bay leaves and serve it hot or warm, with rice, if you like, mango chutney, and eggplant smoor.

> **COOKING NOTE** You can taste seasoned ground beef before you cook it to make sure it has enough salt: heat a little neutral oil in the pan and fry a nugget of the beef mixture in it, taste, and adjust the mixture's seasoning as needed

LAMB SHOULDER
+
DATE
+
CHICKPEAS

Separately, musky lamb, sugary dates, and hearty chickpeas can hold their own. Together, they'd probably be identified as characters in a Middle Eastern culinary plot. But they're longtime players in the North African and Spanish food scenes and shouldn't be confined to a single cuisine, Mediterranean or otherwise.

	CHARACTER	SUBSTITUTE	TIP	COMPLEMENTS
LAMB SHOULDER	Earthy, grassy, sweet	Lamb shank, leg, or neck, pork shoulder, bone-in short rib, chuck roast, brisket, oxtails	Pasture-raised lambs from New Zealand are purely grass-fed and taste gamier than those from America.	Mint, eggplant, peas, parsnips, apricots (dried or fresh), olives, potatoes, lentils, couscous, feta, anchovies
DATE	Sweet, sticky, chewy	Figs (fresh or dried), prunes, jujubes	Try date syrup as an alternative to maple syrup, honey, agave nectar, or molasses.	Coffee, toffee, celery, grain salads, oats, coconut, nuts, sharp or salty cheeses, duck, bacon
CHICKPEAS	Nutty, grainy, firm	Edamame, black beans, cannellini, lima beans, Great Northern beans	They're great roasted; their canned liquid is an egg substitute; and chickpea flour is gluten-free.	Spinach, tomato, stews, soups, dried red chili flakes, couscous, pasta, canned tuna, shellfish, chorizo

Back in the fourth grade, my class studied the Bedouins, and we were each assigned to write about an aspect of nomadic life in the Middle Eastern deserts. I reported on customs. At the end of the quarter, we had a Bedouin-ish potluck to celebrate. My mother made a lamb and apricot pilaf that I subsequently requested from her all the time. Although I developed this uncustomary adaptation in honor of Mom, I took the opportunity to correct a minor imperfection in her recipe: the rice would always come out mushy. I parboil it, then, when it's time to finish it with the braised lamb, I follow a technique similar to that used for Persian *tah dig* (see page 88) so the grains stay firm.

LAMB, DATE & CHICKPEA PILAF

serves 4 to 6

½ teaspoon ground ginger

½ teaspoon ground cumin

3½ teaspoons salt, plus more to taste

1 teaspoon ground white pepper

1¼ pounds deboned lamb shoulder meat, cut into 1½-inch cubes

5 tablespoons unsalted butter

1 cup chopped onion

1 clove garlic, finely chopped

1 cup dates, each pitted and cut into thirds, plus 6 dates, each pitted and cut into sixths

3 tablespoons golden raisins

½ teaspoon ground cinnamon

1 teaspoon orange zest

1½ cups basmati rice

1 (15-ounce) can chickpeas, drained and rinsed

¼ cup chopped fresh mint

Harissa or mango chutney, for serving

Combine the ginger, cumin, 1¼ teaspoons of the salt, and ½ teaspoon of the white pepper in a small bowl. Place the lamb in a large bowl and sprinkle the spice mixture over it, using your hands to toss the lamb and coat the cubes evenly.

In a medium Dutch oven, melt 1 tablespoon of the butter over medium heat. Add the onion and garlic, and sauté, stirring often, until softened and beginning to turn golden, 6 to 8 minutes. Add the lamb and cook, turning repeatedly, until browned on all sides, about 6 minutes. Add the cup of dates, the raisins, and enough water to cover the contents of the pot. Increase the heat to medium-high and bring to a boil, then reduce the heat to medium-low. Add the cinnamon and ½ teaspoon of the orange zest, and simmer, covered, until the meat is tender, 1 to 1¼ hours.

About 20 minutes before the meat is done, make the rice. Using a sieve or colander, rinse the rice under cold water until the water runs clear. Meanwhile, bring 3 cups water to a boil in a large saucepan. When the water is boiling, add 1½ teaspoons of the salt, followed by the rinsed rice. Cook the rice for 5 to 6 minutes, until the grains are just starting to turn opaque and still partially translucent. While the rice is cooking, melt the remaining 4 tablespoons butter. Drain the rice, transfer it to a medium bowl, and stir in the melted butter.

When the lamb is tender, turn off the heat and, using a slotted spoon, transfer the meat, dates, and vegetables (i.e., stew) to a medium bowl, leaving the liquid in the pot. Give the stew a stir; the dates, which will have expanded and softened, will collapse and act as a binder. Add the remaining ¾ teaspoon salt and ½ teaspoon white pepper, and stir again to incorporate.

(recipe continues)

Drain the pot and return it to the stove over medium heat. Add half of the rice and layer the lamb mixture on top. Cover the stew with the remaining rice. Using the handle of a wooden spoon, poke five holes in the pilaf down to the bottom of the pot. Wrap the lid of the pot in a clean kitchen towel, cover the pilaf, and cook until steam emerges from the pot, 5 to 10 minutes; you are likely to hear it hiss. Reduce the heat to low and cook until the rice is tender, about 30 minutes.

When the rice is done, turn off the heat and add the chickpeas, the remaining dates and orange zest, and the fresh mint. Stir together, combining the rice from the bottom. If any rice is stuck to the base of the pot, use your spoon to scrape it up and incorporate it. Taste and add salt as needed. Serve hot with harissa or chutney.

This warming, everything-in-the-pot stew is loosely based on a southern Indian side dish known as *ishtu*—very loosely. In the state of Kerala, where it originated, it's vegetarian and made with regular potatoes. Not mine! This one has lamb and sweet potatoes, because I love the interplay of those ingredients with coconut milk. The spinach stirred in at the end makes for a well-balanced meal. Toss canned chickpeas with toasted, ground spices, fresh herbs, lemon, and dates and you've got a TKO punch of an accompaniment. Less expensive than other cuts, lamb shoulder has more flavor and better proportions of fat and flesh than what's typically marked "stew meat." It's worth seeking out from your butcher.

KERALA-STYLE LAMB STEW

serves 3 or 4

STEW

1 (13½-ounce) can full-fat unsweetened coconut milk, chilled

1 pound deboned lamb shoulder meat, cut into 2-inch pieces

2½ teaspoons salt

2 tablespoons unrefined coconut oil

1 teaspoon whole black peppercorns

6 whole cloves

½ teaspoon allspice berries

2 dried bay leaves

1 medium yellow onion, halved and thickly sliced

1 (2-inch-long) chunk fresh ginger, peeled and cut into matchsticks

2 medium or 3 small green Thai or serrano chilies, halved lengthwise

2 medium sweet potatoes, peeled and cut into 1-inch chunks

1 teaspoon lime zest

2 tablespoons unseasoned rice vinegar

1 bunch fresh spinach (about ½ pound)

Cooked rice or couscous, for serving (optional)

CHICKPEAS

2½ teaspoons coriander seeds

1 teaspoon cumin seeds

½ teaspoon freshly ground black pepper

¼ teaspoon freshly grated nutmeg

2 (15-ounce) cans chickpeas, drained and rinsed

2 tablespoons fresh lemon juice

1 teaspoon salt

¼ cup chopped pitted dates

¼ cup chopped fresh cilantro

¼ cup chopped fresh mint leaves

Make the stew. Use a spoon to scoop out the cream that has risen to the top of the can of coconut milk and set it aside, reserving the liquid milk in the can.

Season the lamb with 1 teaspoon of the salt.

Heat the coconut oil in a medium Dutch oven over medium heat. When the oil is shimmering, add the peppercorns, cloves, allspice, and bay leaves, and cook until fragrant, about 2 minutes. Add the onion, ginger, and chilies, and sauté, stirring often, until softened and browned, 20 to 25 minutes. Add the lamb and sweet potatoes, and continue to sauté, turning constantly, until the meat firms up and its exterior turns gray, about 5 minutes. Add ½ cup plus 1 tablespoon water, ½ teaspoon of the salt, and the reserved coconut milk, and bring to a boil. Reduce the heat to medium-low, add the lime zest, and cover the pot. Simmer until the lamb is tender and cooked through, 1 to 1½ hours.

Meanwhile, prepare the chickpeas. Heat a cast-iron skillet on the stove, gradually increasing the heat from low to medium. Add the coriander seeds and toast them, shaking the pan continuously, until they release a citrusy, popcorn-like aroma and begin to tremble, 2 to 3 minutes. Transfer the seeds to a mortar. Return the skillet to the stove over medium heat and add the cumin seeds, toasting them the same way, until they release their earthier fragrance, up to 1 minute. Add the seeds to the mortar and let them cool. Using the pestle, grind the toasted seeds into a powder. Transfer to a small bowl, add the pepper and nutmeg, and stir to combine.

In a large bowl, combine the chickpeas with 1 teaspoon of the spice mixture, the lemon juice, and salt. Add the dates and fresh cilantro and mint leaves, and stir again to incorporate.

Whisk the coconut cream into the lamb, then add the vinegar and ¾ teaspoon of the salt. Stir in the spinach to coat, and simmer, uncovered, just until wilted, about 5 minutes. Season with the remaining ¼ teaspoon salt. Pick out and discard the whole spices before serving.

Serve the stew hot over plain rice or couscous, if desired, with the chickpeas alongside.

COOKING NOTE Store the leftover spice mixture in a plastic bag or small glass jar wherever you keep your dry spices. It's best used right away but will keep for at least 1 month. Use it to roast vegetables like carrots, parsnips, or butternut squash.

Anyone who's familiar with Korean food knows about *bossam*, a dish of pork belly that's boiled in a garlicky, gingery brine and served in lettuce wraps with a buffet of garnishes. Many Americans have been made aware of it courtesy of David Chang, a Korean American chef who put it on the menu at Momofuku Ssäm Bar, in New York. His is a cured, caramel-crusted, slow-roasted pork butt or shoulder, its glistening flesh disintegrating into its fat. Ever since my first bite, I'd pondered trying something similar on lamb. My rub is a *sui generis* salmagundi of espresso powder, spices, and date syrup, and, with shawarma on the brain, I pack the meat into a pita, with a madcap hummus made to match the lamb's seasonings.

ROASTED LAMB PITAS
WITH HUMMUS
makes 6 sandwiches

LAMB

1 (6- to-7-pound) bone-in lamb shoulder, with some fat cap still attached

2 tablespoons fine sea salt

1 teaspoon freshly ground black pepper

2 teaspoons instant espresso powder

1 teaspoon fennel seeds

3 tablespoons extra-virgin olive oil

2 tablespoons date syrup

5 cloves garlic, finely chopped

3 tablespoons fresh thyme leaves

HUMMUS

1 (15-ounce) can chickpeas, drained and rinsed

1 tablespoon almond butter

1 clove garlic, crushed

2 tablespoons fresh lemon juice

½ teaspoon smoked paprika

½ teaspoon ground cinnamon

½ teaspoon fine sea salt, plus more to taste

3 tablespoons extra-virgin olive oil

¼ cup chopped dates

2 tablespoons sesame seeds, toasted

Pita or flatbread, for serving

Fresh watercress or greens of your choice, for serving

Hot sauce or vinegar, for drizzling (optional)

Prepare the lamb. Lightly score the fat on the lamb in a criss-cross pattern at 1-inch intervals. Place the meat in a large roasting pan. In a small bowl, combine the salt, pepper, espresso powder, and fennel seeds. Generously season the lamb with the spice mixture, coating it evenly on all sides.

In a separate small bowl, whisk together the olive oil and date syrup. Add the garlic and thyme. Using your hands, rub the marinade into the meat, coating it completely. Place the lamb, fat-side up, in the roasting pan. Cover the pan tightly with foil, and chill for at least 2 hours or, preferably, overnight.

Remove the roasting pan from the refrigerator and let the lamb rest at room temperature, keeping it covered with the foil, for 1 hour or so.

Preheat the oven to 325°F.

Roast the lamb, still covered, basting it every 30 minutes and adding ¼ cup water at a time if the pan is dry, until the lamb is tender and pulling easily away from the bones, 4½ to 5 hours. Be sure to resecure the foil tightly between each basting.

Meanwhile, make the hummus. Puree the chickpeas, almond butter, garlic, lemon juice, spices, and salt with 2 tablespoons cold water in a food processor. With the motor running, slowly stream in the olive oil. Pulse until the mixture is smooth, about 1 minute. Transfer the hummus to a small bowl and stir in the dates and sesame seeds to combine. Taste and add salt as needed. This hummus can be stored, covered, in the refrigerator for up to 5 days.

Uncover the lamb, turn the oven to broil, and continue cooking the lamb, basting it halfway through, until its fat is golden brown and crisp, about 3 minutes total, or, if you prefer, beginning to char, 4 to 5 minutes.

Transfer the lamb to a cutting board and let it rest for at least 20 minutes. Skim and discard the fat from the surface of the juices in the roasting pan. Reserve the remaining juices in a pitcher or small bowl.

To serve, slather each pita with the hummus, pile on some of the lamb, and garnish with watercress. Spoon some of the reserved lamb gravy on top or add any hot sauce or vinegar you like.

PORK BELLY
+
PRUNE
+
RADICCHIO

Most Americans know pork belly as a cured and smoked substance called bacon. Recently, we've embraced it, fresh, with its irresistible (sometimes even to vegetarians) sheath of fat that keeps its flesh succulent. It's almost too sumptuous, but here it is reined in by the bitterness of purple-speckled radicchio and the caramel sweetness of prunes.

	CHARACTER	SUBSTITUTE	TIP	COMPLEMENTS
PORK BELLY	Rich, meaty, meltingly tender	Lamb belly, pork shoulder, pork or beef cheeks	Ask your butcher for a leaner piece of center-cut belly. Look for heritage Berkshire pork.	Caramel, apples, stone fruit, scallions, broccoli rabe, arugula, cannellini, lentils, chestnuts, anchovies, oysters
PRUNE	Caramel, soft, plump	Dried cherries, figs, apricots; dates, raisins	Prunes are semi-dried, so they're relatively hydrated and don't need to be reconstituted before cooking.	Warm spices, orange, shallots, chocolate, brandy, heavy cream, yogurt, chestnuts, almonds, goat cheese, bacon
RADICCHIO	Bitter, crisp, chicory	Endive, frisée, escarole, dandelion greens	Roast it! Drizzle wedges with olive oil, season with salt and pepper, and cook in a 450°F oven.	Balsamic, grapes, citrus, cannellini, lentils, risotto, almonds, hazelnuts, walnuts, blue cheese, Parmesan, salmon, bacon

Shogayaki is a popular Japanese home-style dish of gingery pork (sometimes beef) grilled—or stir-fried—with soy sauce and sweet mirin; usually, it's served with shredded cabbage. I've led the pig down another flavor path, but I've honored the original tenets: a quickie marinade that's cooked with the meat and becomes the dressing for the lettuce, a limited number of ingredients, and all-around ease. In Japan, a small bowl of *tsukemono*, or pickles, might be offered on the side, with rice, or as a garnish. I brined some prunes to go with the belly; they'd also be bonkers with roasts.

STIR-FRIED PORK BELLY
WITH PICKLED PRUNES

serves 4

PICKLED PRUNES

½ naval orange

1 pound pitted prunes

1 cup red wine vinegar

½ cup packed light brown sugar

½ cup honey

½ teaspoon dried thyme

4 allspice berries

1 teaspoon yellow mustard seeds

¼ teaspoon dried red chili flakes

Salt to taste

PORK

2 tablespoons unseasoned rice vinegar

1½ tablespoons honey

1 tablespoon hoisin sauce

1 tablespoon Dijon mustard

2 tablespoons soy sauce

1 teaspoon finely chopped fresh rosemary leaves

1 shallot, roughly chopped

¼ teaspoon freshly ground black pepper, plus more to taste

1¼ pounds boneless, skinless pork belly, cut into ¼-inch-thick slices

1 medium head radicchio

2 tablespoons finely chopped fresh chives

1 teaspoon fresh thyme leaves

1 tablespoon neutral oil

1 lemon, quartered

Salt to taste

Pickle the prunes. Before juicing the orange, peel its zest in long thin strips. In a medium heavy-bottomed saucepan, combine the orange zest and juice, prunes, red wine vinegar, brown sugar, honey, thyme, allspice, mustard seeds, chili flakes, and salt. Bring to a boil over medium-high heat. Reduce the heat to medium and continue to cook for 15 minutes, stirring from time to time, to allow the flavors to intensify. Reduce the heat to low and simmer until the liquid has thickened substantially, becoming syrupy, up to 10 minutes more. (If the prunes seem in danger of falling apart, use a slotted spoon to transfer them to a plate while you reduce the liquid, then return them to the saucepan when the liquid is done.) Remove the saucepan from the stove and let the prunes cool to room temperature. Transfer them, with their liquid, to a sealed container. They will keep in the fridge for at least 2 weeks. Serve cold or at room temperature.

Prepare the pork. In a medium bowl, whisk together the vinegar, honey, hoisin, mustard, and soy sauce. Whisk in the rosemary and shallot, followed by the black pepper.

Add the pork to the marinade, turning to coat. Cover the bowl with plastic wrap and marinate for 15 to 20 minutes at room temperature.

Meanwhile, trim and shred the radicchio. Transfer to a serving bowl. Add the chives and thyme and toss to incorporate.

Heat a large cast-iron skillet gradually on the stove, increasing the heat from low to high. Add the oil. When the oil is shimmering, add the pork to the pan, using tongs or a slotted spoon, reserving the marinade, and sauté until browned on both sides, about 4 minutes total. Add the marinade to the pan and continue to cook, stirring occasionally, until the sauce begins to caramelize and coats the meat, about 4 minutes more.

Transfer the pork to a serving plate and spoon the marinade sauce over the radicchio, tossing to incorporate. Squeeze the lemon over both the meat and the salad. Season both with a pinch or two of salt and a couple grinds of pepper. Taste and adjust the seasoning as needed. Serve immediately with the pickled prunes alongside.

Have you ever been to a dinner party where the host plonks a Dutch oven full of what looks, smells, and tastes like heaven on the table, and tells you all he did was chuck everything in the pot, put the lid on, and leave it in the oven? You assume his nonchalance is an act and he slaved over the stove. I have news for you: he may have been telling the truth. As this dunce-proof recipe for pork belly slowly sweltered in a bottle of wine with prunes and radicchio shows, you can, in fact, make a one-pot dish that is simultaneously humble and dramatic without any heavy lifting, except for the maneuvering of the cooking vessel.

BRAISED PORK BELLY
WITH PRUNES & RADICCHIO

serves 4

1 (2¼-pound) piece boneless, skin-on pork belly

½ teaspoon salt, plus more to taste

¼ teaspoon freshly ground black pepper, plus more to taste

2 tablespoons extra-virgin olive oil

2 large carrots, peeled and cut into 2 × ¼-inch batons

1 large onion, roughly chopped

¾ cup pitted prunes (4 to 5 ounces), halved

7 (⅛-inch-thick) slices unpeeled ginger

4 whole star anise

1 (750 ml) bottle dry white wine

1 tablespoon dark soy sauce

3½ tablespoons sugar

1 head radicchio, cored and cut into 5 or 6 wedges

Preheat the oven to 350°F.

Season the skin of the pork with the salt and pepper, massaging it in.

Heat the olive oil in a medium Dutch oven over medium heat. When the oil is shimmering, add the pork, skin-side down. Cook it until the skin is browned, about 10 minutes. Remove the pot from the heat and transfer the pork to a plate.

Add the carrots, onion, prunes, ginger, star anise, wine, soy sauce, and sugar to the pot. Return the pork to the pot, skin-side up, and cover. Transfer the pot to the oven, basting it every 30 minutes, and cook until the meat is meltingly tender, about 2½ hours.

Remove the lid and add the radicchio, placing it around the pork. Baste some of the cooking liquid over the wedges. Return the pot to the oven, uncovered, and cook until the radicchio is cooked through and wilted and the liquid has become a dark, glossy sauce, 30 minutes more.

Remove the pot from the oven and transfer the pork to a cutting board to rest for 15 minutes, keeping the pot covered so the vegetables stay warm. Discard the star anise and ginger. Season the vegetables and sauce with salt and pepper as needed. Slice the pork and transfer the pieces to the pot, placing them on top of the vegetables. Serve hot.

I was at my desk, ravenous, when I saw an Instagram photo of a mound of burgundy-streaked radicchio with morsels of near-black dried purple plum and crumbly white feta peeking out. It evoked stabs of hunger and jealousy. I forwarded the picture to a prune-loving friend, who replicated the salad and reported it "was like a mouth orgasm." Clearly, I had to try it. Ever the lily-gilder, I added pork belly, applying a technique for roasting the meat so the flesh goes tender, the fat collapsing, and the skin gets so crunchy it shatters like brittle or a crème brûlée crust. Then I shook up a feisty, tart vinaigrette in a jar, my preferred method for making (and vessel for storing) dressing.

RADICCHIO, PRUNE & PORK BELLY SALAD

serves 4 as an appetizer

- 1½ pounds boneless, skin-on pork belly
- ½ teaspoon fine sea salt, plus more to taste
- ½ teaspoon freshly ground black pepper, plus more to taste
- Boiling water
- 1 large head Treviso or round radicchio, roughly chopped into bite-size pieces
- ¼ pound feta, crumbled (about 1 cup)
- ¾ cup pitted prunes, quartered
- 2 tablespoons roughly chopped fresh mint
- 2 tablespoons roughly chopped fresh cilantro
- 4 tablespoons Lime Vinaigrette (recipe follows)

Preheat the oven to 400°F.

Blot the pork skin dry with paper towels, then rub it all over with the salt and pepper. Place the pork, skin-side up, on a rack in a deep roasting pan, then, avoiding the meat, pour in enough boiling water to come just below the rack. Roast the pork, refilling the water as needed to keep it level, until the skin is crisp and the meat is tender, 1½ to 1¾ hours. Remove from the oven, transfer the pork to a cutting board, and let it rest for about 15 minutes.

Meanwhile, place the radicchio in a large bowl and season it with a pinch of salt and pepper. Toss to combine. Add the crumbled feta and toss again, followed by the prunes. Sprinkle in the fresh mint and cilantro and toss. Drizzle 3 tablespoons of the vinaigrette around the perimeter of the salad as you toss, folding everything from the edge toward the middle to coat evenly.

Cut the rested pork into bite-size cubes and add them to the salad. Drizzle the belly pieces with the remaining 1 tablespoon vinaigrette and toss again to incorporate.

LIME VINAIGRETTE

Makes about ½ cup

- 3 tablespoons fresh lime juice
- 1 tablespoon unseasoned rice vinegar
- 2 teaspoons Dijon mustard
- 2 teaspoons pomegranate molasses
- ¼ teaspoon ground sumac
- ¼ cup extra-virgin olive oil, plus more as needed
- ¼ teaspoon salt, plus more to taste
- Freshly ground black pepper to taste
- Lime zest to taste

Combine the lime juice, rice vinegar, Dijon mustard, pomegranate molasses, and sumac in a small glass jar, put the lid on, and shake to combine. Add the olive oil and repeat. Taste and add more olive oil, if needed, shaking again to incorporate. Season with the salt and pepper, and give it another shake to incorporate. Add a few gratings of lime zest to the jar and shake to combine. Give it a final taste and if you want to add more of anything, do so now, shaking the vinaigrette to incorporate. Covered, it will keep in the refrigerator for up to 3 days. You will need to shake it again before serving, as it separates.

DAIRY

EGGS
+
OLIVES
+
LABNEH

Even when meat and money are scarce, you can still scare up a few eggs and, with them, a complete meal. Brined fruity olives and the creamy Middle Eastern yogurt cheese known as labneh aren't really things you cook; they're things you *cook with*, to make more of what you've got.

	CHARACTER	SUBSTITUTE	TIP	COMPLEMENTS
EGGS	Silky, oozy, fluffy	If they're the center of a dish, there is no substitute. But why not try duck eggs?	Fresh eggs sink to the bottom in a bowl of cold water. Dump the floaters.	Bread, heavy cream, cheese, smoked salmon, bacon, ham, sausage, salami, steak, chicken liver
OLIVES	Salty, bracing, meaty	Capers, caperberries, pickled vegetables like Japanese *oshinko*, sun-dried tomatoes, anchovies	If they're too assertive, rinse them off. Deep-brown niçoise olives are a good all-purpose choice.	Herbs, garlic, nightshades, cornmeal, pasta, mozzarella, goat cheese, feta, ricotta, fish, chicken, lamb
LABNEH	Tangy, cooling, dense	Greek yogurt, skyr, cream cheese, mascarpone, quark, sour cream, crème fraîche, fresh goat cheese	DIY by straining 2 pounds high-quality yogurt mixed with ½ teaspoon salt through a muslin-lined sieve.	Herbs, spices, extra-virgin olive oil, jam, garlic, sun-dried tomatoes, bread, smoked salmon

I've said it before and I'll say it again: when it comes to egg salad, let your yolks do the work—cut down on the mayonnaise. You want velvety-rich, luscious material with sandwich potential, not wet, mushy, melts-in-the-heat-of-the-day-and-reeks-like-sulfur slop. That means less binder, and a better one—enter labneh, with its tart, dense cream-cheesiness. Let this recipe be your template, even if you stay the mayo course. If you follow the directions as written, you can enjoy my egg salad with a fork or allow it to live up to its promise between two slices of brioche, Pullman, pumpernickel, or focaccia, with some watercress or arugula tucked in—and maybe just a teensy bit more honey mustard spread on the bread.

EGG SALAD

*makes enough for
4 sandwiches*

6 large eggs

5 tablespoons labneh

2½ teaspoons honey mustard

Salt and freshly ground black pepper to taste

½ cup pitted picholine olives, roughly chopped

¼ cup toasted pistachios or almonds, roughly chopped

1½ teaspoons finely chopped fresh rosemary

2 teaspoons roughly chopped fresh chervil (see Substitution Note)

2 teaspoons finely chopped fresh chives

Place the eggs in a large pot and add enough water to cover by ¾ inch. Cook over high heat, stirring occasionally, until just before the water starts to boil, 15 to 20 minutes. Remove the pot from the heat, cover, and let the eggs sit for 9 minutes.

Meanwhile, stir together the labneh and honey mustard in a medium bowl.

Drain the eggs and run them under cold water to stop the cooking. Peel them and separate the whites and yolks. Use your hands to break up the whites and place them in a small bowl. Put the yolks in the bowl with the labneh and honey mustard. Using a fork, smash the yolks into the honey mustard mixture to form a paste and season it with salt and pepper. Fold in the egg whites, olives, and pistachios, evenly combining and fluffing the salad as you go. Gently fold in the rosemary, chervil, and chives. Taste and adjust the seasoning as needed. Combine and fluff again, taking care not to overwork the salad. It's ready to serve.

SUBSTITUTION NOTE Chervil's leaves are small and pretty. They taste like a milder tarragon crossed with parsley. You can substitute those for this herb, or choose others you like—basil, dill, or thyme, for example.

The first thing I ever cooked by myself was my father's specialty, scrambled eggs, which I proudly made for him. Dad's continued to be voted the best in the family for the next two decades. That changed when I learned the slow scramble, or French-style method, which entails cooking the eggs over indirect heat—in a double boiler—while constantly agitating them with a whisk to keep them soft and creamy. A lump of butter to finish helps. Cheffy types artfully blend in crème fraîche, but I've switched over to labneh; it has the silkiness of the former with a sharper, saltier flavor. That's what eggs need: flavor—and seasoning. Enter olive tapenade, one that puts the fruit first and sesame, sumac, and marjoram second.

SLOW-SCRAMBLED EGGS
WITH OLIVE TAPENADE

serves 4

12 large eggs

Salt and freshly ground black pepper to taste

¼ cup labneh

2 tablespoons (¼ stick) unsalted butter, softened

Olive Tapenade (recipe follows or store-bought), for serving

Toast, for serving (optional)

Bring water to a simmer in the base of a double boiler (see Cooking Notes, page 109).

Meanwhile, crack the eggs into a large bowl and season with salt and pepper. Whisk until frothy. Add the labneh and whisk to incorporate.

Add the beaten eggs to the top of the double boiler. Cook gradually, whisking vigorously, nonstop. Just as they begin to set and form curds, which takes at least 10 minutes, remove the top pot from the heat; the eggs should have the texture of cottage cheese. Whisk in the butter.

Spoon the scrambled eggs into 4 bowls or onto plates, swirling 1½ to 2 teaspoons olive tapenade into the hot eggs. Serve with toast, if desired.

OLIVE TAPENADE
Makes ⅜ cup

½ cup pitted niçoise and/or kalamata black olives, roughly chopped

1 small clove garlic, minced

2 tablespoons loosely packed fresh marjoram or oregano leaves

1 tablespoon sesame seeds, toasted

1 teaspoon ground sumac

1 teaspoon fresh lemon juice

2 tablespoons extra-virgin olive oil

Kosher salt and freshly ground black pepper to taste

Combine the olives, garlic, marjoram, sesame seeds, and sumac in a mortar. Using the pestle, gradually break down the ingredients to create a paste. (Note: You can do this in a food processor, if preferred.) Work in the lemon juice, then drizzle in the olive oil to make it spreadable. Season with salt and pepper. Taste and adjust the seasoning as needed. Store, covered, in the refrigerator for up to 1 week.

Of the many ways you can cook eggs, I believe baking them has the gentlest learning curve and highest success rate. Prepared this way, they're nearly impossible to screw up. You can crack them into homemade tomato sauce, heavy cream, or ricotta, with pancetta, Parmesan, spinach, bread crumbs, herbs, or olives. I put the latter in mine, choosing the large, green Castelvetranos from Sicily, and cook them in labneh. You'll see baked eggs on lots of restaurant brunch menus; they arrive straight from the oven, often in small gratin dishes so each diner has her own. That's how I do it at home, whether I'm fixing myself a light supper or feeding a loved one or two. Fifteen minutes is all you need.

LABNEH-BAKED EGGS

serves 1

3 tablespoons labneh

½ teaspoon harissa

2 large eggs

Salt and freshly ground
    black pepper to taste

2 Castelvetrano olives, pitted
    and torn into pieces (see
    Substitution Note)

Fresh thyme leaves and chopped
    fresh basil, flat-leaf parsley,
    or oregano, for garnish

Preheat the oven to 375°F.

In a small bowl, whisk together the labneh and harissa using a fork.

Crack 2 eggs into a mini gratin dish, taking care not to break the yolks. Gently place dollops of the labneh mixture around the eggs, filling the surface area of the dish, and sprinkle with a generous pinch of salt and pepper. Dot the dish with the olive pieces.

Bake until the whites are just set and the yolks are very loose, 9 to 10 minutes; the eggs will continue to cook once they're out of the oven.

Garnish with a generous showering of fresh herbs before serving.

> **SUBSTITUTION NOTE** Castelvetranos are larger than most olives. Picholines are smaller but equally well suited here; use an extra one per serving.

GOAT CHEESE
+
STRAWBERRY
+
BALSAMIC

Strawberries become a better-than-sour-candy version of themselves when combined with balsamic vinegar, and salty, tangy goat cheese gets on with that slightly sweet, acidic liquid like a house on fire. So it stands to reason that the berries and chèvre also benefit from each other's company. It's a culinary syllogism—and a sound one.

	CHARACTER	SUBSTITUTE	TIP	COMPLEMENTS
GOAT CHEESE	Tangy, earthy, crumbly	Feta, mascarpone, ricotta, cream cheese, or a combination (for fresh); Camembert or Brie (for aged)	Fresh is soft and mild; aged is stronger, with a weepy outer layer and denser center.	Greens, leeks, sweet bell peppers, eggplant, fruit (fresh or dried), honey, nuts, chicken, bacon, sausage
STRAWBERRY	Sweet, tart, juicy	Any other fresh berry or combination of berries; dried strawberries, strawberry jam, pickled strawberries	The best are local, in-season, red (not green or white) and really smell like strawberries.	Herbs, spinach, citrus, stone fruit, rhubarb, ginger, coconut, sesame, black pepper, cream, almonds, pistachios, halloumi
BALSAMIC	Mellow, fruity, acidic	Sherry, apple cider, red wine, or saba vinegar (add honey or sugar as needed)	The best are from Modena, Italy, and marked IGP. Darker balsamics are sweeter.	Fruit, ice cream, roasted vegetables, fresh mozzarella, Parmesan, grilled or roasted pork or chicken, duck

Whoever has prepacked parfaits into sad, flimsy plastic cups and stacked them in the refrigerated cases of airport kiosks has participated in a smear campaign against the layered compositions I once loved. As of right now, I'm restoring their good name, starting with this striated dessert of macerated berries smothered in a cloud of creamy soft goat cheese, drizzled with viscous balsamic, and strewn with crumbly crunchies. Eat it seconds after it's been piled into a bowl or sundae glass, plunging your spoon to the bottom so it can catch some of each element in one bite.

STRAWBERRIES
WITH WHIPPED GOAT CHEESE & BALSAMIC SYRUP

serves 6

2 pounds fresh strawberries, hulled and sliced about ¼ inch thick

½ cup honey

2 tablespoons fresh lemon juice

4 sprigs fresh mint

1⅓ cups balsamic vinegar

2½ tablespoons packed light brown sugar

8 ounces fresh goat cheese (1 cup), at room temperature

½ cup heavy cream

1½ tablespoons strawberry jam

Kosher salt to taste

TOPPINGS

½ cup toasted hazelnuts, pistachios, and/or almonds, roughly chopped; or

Butter cookies, crumbled

Macerate the strawberries. In a large bowl, toss the strawberries with the honey and lemon juice until the liquids combine and coat all the berries. Submerge the mint sprigs into the mixture, cover the bowl with plastic wrap, and place it in the fridge for at least 30 minutes or up to 24 hours.

Make the balsamic syrup. In a small heavy-bottomed saucepan, bring the balsamic vinegar and brown sugar to a boil over medium heat. Cook, stirring occasionally, until the liquid reduces to ½ cup and is just beginning to thicken, about 25 minutes. Be sure the vinegar doesn't burn or the mixture become too viscous—if it's too thick, it will seize up as it cools and become solid. Remove the syrup from the heat and let it cool before using. Stored in a sealed container, it will keep in the refrigerator for up to a month. Serve at room temperature.

Make the whipped goat cheese. In a stand mixer fitted with the paddle (or using a medium bowl and handheld electric mixer), whip the goat cheese and cream together on medium speed until smooth, creamy, and aerated. Add the strawberry jam and continue to mix until incorporated. Season with a pinch of salt. Transfer to a small bowl. Stored in a sealed container, it will keep in the refrigerator for up to 4 days.

To serve, remove the mint sprigs from the strawberries and discard the herb. Using a slotted spoon, evenly divide the berries among 6 bowls. Top each with a hefty dollop (2 heaping spoonfuls) of the whipped goat cheese and drizzle up to 1 teaspoon of the balsamic syrup on top. Garnish with 1 tablespoon chopped nuts per bowl or some crumbled butter cookies.

The first time I went to Le Coucou restaurant in Manhattan, I was so distracted by how cinematic the cavernous space was that I barely paid attention to what was being ordered. Then a plate bearing a trail of strawberries and small tomatoes was set down, and its pretty simplicity caught my eye. Once tasted, the pairing held my attention. What impressed me, aside from how well the two red fruits got on together, was that both were out of season, and the dish seemed better for it. For the first time, I appreciated the sourness of the berries and the muted acidity of the tomatoes. I've done something less minimalist with that combination, using goat cheese to keep the original dish's flavors at the fore.

STRAWBERRY TOMATO SALAD

serves 4

12 ounces strawberries, hulled and quartered (about 2¼ cups)

12 ounces cherry tomatoes, halved (about 2¼ cups)

1 medium cucumber, quartered lengthwise and cut into ½-inch slices (about 2 cups)

½ teaspoon flake salt, plus more to taste

¼ teaspoon freshly ground black pepper

¼ pound Bûcheron or other semi-aged goat cheese, cubed

3 tablespoons roughly chopped fresh basil

1 tablespoon roughly chopped fresh tarragon

1 tablespoon balsamic vinegar

¼ teaspoon honey

3 tablespoons extra-virgin olive oil

In a large serving bowl, toss together the strawberries, tomatoes, cucumber, salt, and pepper. Add the goat cheese and gently toss again, just to incorporate. Add the herbs and toss quickly to distribute.

In a small bowl, whisk together the balsamic vinegar and honey using a fork. Continuing to whisk, slowly stream in the olive oil to form a vinaigrette.

Pour the vinaigrette over the salad and toss to combine. Taste and add salt as needed. It's ready to go.

"Strawberry shortcake, banana split, we think your team's a bucket of . . . Shift to the left, shift to the right . . . !" To this day, even when I'm enjoying a flawlessly executed strawberry shortcake with the juiciest berries and tenderest-crumbed biscuit, I hear that summer-camp sports cheer. The quaint red-and-white dessert, perhaps more American even than apple pie, is perfect as is. But I wanted to shift it, just a little. When I tasted my handiwork, I cheered real loud. Faced with crappy fresh fruit, you shouldn't feel bad about buying a jar of good strawberry jam and spooning it onto the shortcakes. And when peaches are in season, you shouldn't beat yourself up for putting the stone fruit in the starting lineup.

STRAWBERRY SHORTCAKE

serves 4

2 ounces fresh goat cheese

1¼ cups all-purpose flour, plus more as needed

¼ cup plus 3 tablespoons granulated sugar

1 teaspoon baking powder

¼ teaspoon salt

¾ teaspoon freshly ground black pepper

5½ tablespoons unsalted butter, cut into ½-inch cubes and chilled

¼ cup heavy cream, plus more as needed and for brushing

1½ pounds strawberries (2 pints), hulled and cut lengthwise into ⅛-inch slices

1 vanilla bean, split and scraped, pod reserved

2 tablespoons balsamic vinegar

Demerara or turbinado sugar, for sprinkling (optional)

Vanilla ice cream or unsweetened fresh whipped cream, for serving

Put the goat cheese in the freezer for 5 minutes to firm up. Remove it from the freezer and cut it into ½-inch cubes. Put it back in the freezer to firm up again while you gather and combine your dry ingredients.

In a large bowl, whisk together the flour, ¼ cup of the granulated sugar, the baking powder, salt, and pepper to combine. Working quickly and using your fingers, incorporate the butter and goat cheese cubes by smearing them into the dry mix, one small pile at a time, being sure all of the dry ingredients come into contact with the butter. The butter and cheese will break down into flakes to yield a coarse crumble. (You can also do this with a pastry cutter.)

Slowly stream in the heavy cream. Begin to swirl your hand through the mixture, using your fingers to integrate the wet and dry ingredients and do most of the work of bringing the dough together, then give it a quick knead to form a thoroughly incorporated, sticky dough. You may not need all of the cream; start with ¼ cup, adding more as needed. Alternatively, if the mixture is still too dry, add a bit more cream, as needed, 1 tablespoon at a time.

Turn the dough out onto a lightly floured work surface and pat it into a rectangle about ¾-inch thick. Press—without twisting—a 2½-inch biscuit cutter straight down into the dough to cut out rounds, getting as many as you can out of the dough. Pile the scraps on top of each other in layers and pat them out to form another ¾-inch-thick rectangle to cut more rounds, repeating until there is no dough left; you should have at least 4 shortcakes. Layer them between wax paper and place them in a sealed plastic bag or container to chill while you continue cooking.

Place the berries in a large bowl and sprinkle them with the remaining 3 tablespoons granulated sugar. Toss to coat. Cover and refrigerate for 1 to 4 hours.

Preheat the oven to 375°F.

Remove the strawberries from the refrigerator and gently stir in the vanilla seeds and pod to combine. Stir in the balsamic vinegar, and transfer the berries and their juices into a large ovenproof dish or sauté pan. Roast until the juices are bubbling and the berries are hot but not mushy, 6 to 10 minutes. Remove them from the oven, discard the vanilla pod, and cover the dish with aluminum foil to keep warm. Reduce the oven temperature to 350°F.

Line a baking sheet with parchment paper.

Remove the chilled shortcakes from the refrigerator and transfer them to the prepared baking sheet. Brush each round lightly with heavy cream and, if you like, sprinkle with a pinch of Demerara sugar. Bake until they're just cooked through and their edges are golden, 20 to 25 minutes.

To assemble, split the shortcakes horizontally, placing a bottom half on each of 4 plates, split-side up. Spoon some of the strawberries over each and top the fruit with a generous dollop of ice cream. Spoon some additional juice from the berries over the ice cream and place the top halves of the shortcakes over each pile. Serve immediately.

RICOTTA
+
ORANGE
+
AMARETTI

One should always have bread crumbs around, or something better that can *become* bread crumbs, like almond-flavored Italian amaretti cookies. Same as docile ricotta and vibrant oranges, they are AC/DC ingredients, which means they can go into sweet and—with some salt, heat, and (where that citrus comes in) acid—savory dishes.

	CHARACTER	SUBSTITUTE	TIP	COMPLEMENTS
RICOTTA	Milky, gentle, soft	Mascarpone, fromage frais, fromage blanc, quark, cottage cheese	Smoked ricotta is spectacular, if rare. Use it instead of regular ricotta in savory recipes.	Fresh or roasted fruit, citrus, vanilla, jam
ORANGE	Acidic, sweet, citrus	Grapefruit, Meyer lemon, marmalade	Naval isn't the only orange; give tangerines, clementines, cara caras, or blood oranges a chance!	Fennel, winter squash, figs, olives, prunes, dates, vanilla, pork, chicken, duck
AMARETTI	Sugary, almond, crunchy	Speculoos, gingersnaps, graham crackers, Nilla wafers, animal crackers	Find the red tins marked Lazzaroni Amaretti di Saronno, the best-known brand of these macaroons.	Stone fruit, apples, pears, ice cream, fennel, winter squash, sweet potatoes, radicchio, blue cheese, Parmesan

Pasta and macaroons, how could this be!? It's not an obvious coupling. But if you taste the classic Italian preparation of butter-and-sage-sauced pumpkin-stuffed *lune* garnished with a grating of Parmesan and amaretti, you'll be moonstruck. I conveyed the sweet almond-flavored cookies into an understatedly sophisticated chili-hot pasta that's a lot less work. Its spiciness tempers the sweetness of the amaretti and the orange zest. If you're heat sensitive, skip this one. And if you enjoy setting your mouth on fire, increase the amount of chili flakes (and try using the smoked varietal, too). Ridged penne is an optimal noodle for this recipe, but it's not alone. You can experiment with whatever shape you're into. Keep in mind that grooves and curls catch crumbs and cheese.

WHOLE-WHEAT PASTA
WITH AMARETTI, ORANGE & RICOTTA

serves 4

4½ tablespoons extra-virgin olive oil

8 amaretti cookies, roughly crumbled

1¼ teaspoons salt, plus more to taste

1 pound whole-wheat dried penne

2 teaspoons fennel seeds

3 medium shallots, finely chopped (about 1 cup)

1½ teaspoons dried red chili flakes

2 teaspoons orange zest

1 pound fresh whole-milk ricotta cheese (2 cups)

Flake salt, for sprinkling

Best-quality extra-virgin olive oil, for drizzling

Fresh oregano leaves, for sprinkling (optional)

Heat 1 tablespoon of the olive oil in a large sauté pan over medium-high heat. When the oil is shimmering, add the amaretti crumbs to coat, and toast, tossing frequently, 2 to 3 minutes. Remove the pan from the heat and season the crumbs with ¼ teaspoon of the salt, tasting and adjusting as needed. Transfer ¼ cup plus 2 tablespoons of the crumbs to a bowl and set aside. (Snack on or discard the rest.) Wipe out the pan and set it aside.

Bring 3 quarts water to a boil in a large pot over high heat. When the water is boiling, salt it. Add the pasta, stirring once right after you put it in the pot and then again, a minute later, to prevent sticking. Cook the pasta until al dente. Reserve ½ cup of the pasta cooking water, then drain the penne.

Meanwhile, heat 1½ tablespoons of the olive oil in the reserved sauté pan over medium heat. When the oil is shimmering, add the fennel seeds and toast until fragrant, stirring once or twice, 2 to 3 minutes. Add the shallots and sauté, stir-ring frequently, until soft and translucent, about 5 minutes. Stir in the chili flakes and turn off the heat.

Add the pasta and ¼ cup of the reserved cooking water to the shallots and stir over medium heat to coat, adding a splash or two more of the water as needed to create a light, sauce-like emulsification that evenly coats all of the penne. Stir in the remaining 2 tablespoons olive oil and the orange zest. Season with the remaining 1 teaspoon salt, tasting and adjusting as needed. Stir in ¼ cup of the amaretti crumbs to combine, then sprinkle the remaining 2 tablespoons over the top.

To serve, evenly divide the pasta among 4 bowls and top each with a few globs of the fresh ricotta (about ½ cup per portion). Sprinkle the cheese with flake salt and drizzle with extra-virgin olive oil. If you'd like, garnish with oregano leaves or another fresh herb. Serve hot, instructing guests to stir the cheese into the pasta.

I'm not sure they have sundaes in Italy. The only Italian versions I've had are called *coppetta*, and they're scooped in the United States. My made-in-America Italianate composition starts with an eggless ricotta gelato that reminds me of pre-bedtime warm milk. Its creamy comfort is merrily disrupted by the raucous crunch of semi-salty amaretti crumble and the tintinnabulating tartness of orange curd. How much of each component you add is yours to decide. And you don't need an ice cream maker—just put the gelato base in a very cold metal bowl in the freezer and, after an hour, whisk it every 15 minutes until it has set. If your cheese is extra fresh, you don't have to turn it into ice cream at all.

RICOTTA GELATO COPPETTA

serves 6

GELATO

¾ cup heavy cream

1¾ cups whole milk

1 cinnamon stick

¼ cup sugar

3 heaping tablespoons honey

¼ teaspoon pure almond extract

2 teaspoons amaretto liqueur (optional)

⅜ teaspoon kosher salt

1 pound fresh whole-milk ricotta cheese (2 cups)

ORANGE CURD

¾ cup fresh orange juice (from 2 to 3 oranges)

Zest of 1 orange

1 tablespoon fresh lemon juice

1 large egg

2 large egg yolks

3 tablespoons sugar

1 tablespoon honey

4 tablespoons (½ stick) unsalted butter, cubed and softened

Salt to taste

AMARETTI CRUNCH

3 tablespoons extra-virgin olive oil

1 cup blanched almonds, roughly chopped

2 tablespoons sesame seeds

1 cup crumbled amaretti cookies (about 10 cookies)

¼ teaspoon flake salt, plus more to taste

Make the gelato. Combine the cream, milk, cinnamon stick, sugar, and honey in a medium saucepan over medium heat. Cook, stirring occasionally. When the liquid starts to boil, about 10 minutes, remove the pan from the heat and let it come to room temperature, about 30 minutes.

Strain the cooled mixture through a fine-mesh sieve set over a medium bowl, discarding the cinnamon stick. Stir the almond extract, amaretto (if using), and kosher salt into the liquid. Refrigerate the gelato base in a sealed container for at least 3 hours or overnight.

When the base is chilled, prepare the ricotta. In a large bowl, whisk the ricotta to break up the curds and smooth and soften the overall texture. Take the gelato base from the refrigerator and whisk it into the cheese, breaking up any lumps. Transfer the base to your ice cream maker and follow the manufacturer's instructions for churning ice cream, noting that gelato should take slightly less time. (Check it after 15 minutes and stop it when the gelato has achieved the consistency of a thick milkshake.) The gelato is best enjoyed the day it's made, but will keep for at least a week in a sealed container in the freezer.

Make the curd. Heat the orange juice in a small saucepan over medium-high heat. Bring to a rapid simmer and cook until reduced to ¼ cup, about 7 minutes. Transfer the orange juice to a small bowl to cool to room temperature. Stir in the zest and lemon juice.

In a separate small bowl, whisk together the egg, yolks, sugar, and honey. Whisk the cooled orange juice into the egg mixture in a steady stream.

Pour the egg mixture back into the saucepan over medium heat. Cook, whisking slowly but constantly, being sure to scrape the bottom, until the mixture has thickened to a pudding-like consistency, 5 to 7 minutes (or until a thermometer inserted in the mixture reads 180°F).

Pour the mixture through a strainer set over a small bowl, discarding any solids. Whisk in the butter and salt (up to ¼ teaspoon, tasting and adjusting accordingly). The curd can be refrigerated in a sealed container for up to a week.

Make the amaretti crunch. Heat a large cast-iron skillet on the stove, gradually increasing the heat from low to medium. Add the olive oil. When the oil is shimmering, add the almonds and stir to coat. Toast the nuts,

stirring constantly, until fragrant and light golden brown, 3 to 5 minutes. Add the sesame seeds, continuing to stir, and cook until fragrant and golden, 1 to 2 minutes. Add the amaretti and stir to incorporate and lightly toast, 1 minute. Remove the pan from the heat and season with ¼ teaspoon flake salt, tasting and adjusting as needed. Let cool. Store the crunch in a sealed, paper-towel-lined container at room temperature for up to 3 days.

To assemble, place about 2 spoonfuls of the crunch in the base of a small bowl or coupe-style glass. Add a small scoop of the gelato on top and blanket it with a generous spoonful of curd. Add a second small scoop of gelato and garnish with another 2 spoonfuls or so of the crunch.

SUBSTITUTION NOTE If you don't have time to make the curd, your favorite, not-too-bitter store-bought orange marmalade will do.

Soufflés don't come any easier than this. Neither do cheesecakes. The way I look at it, this soufflé offers a quicker way to make an airier ricotta cheesecake. It's a lovely, floofy cumulus of a thing that you can serve at a dinner party or bake for your family on a weeknight. Put it in the oven before you sit down to eat, and it will be ready in time for dessert. Just don't set your expectations too high for its crown; it's a rustic soufflé and it will rise, but it won't achieve the "top hat" of a classic French model. Alternatively, while those towering textbook beauties deflate in an instant, this soufflé's weightier structure allows it to hold its shape and humble height.

ORANGE-RICOTTA SOUFFLÉ

serves 4 to 6

Unsalted butter, for greasing

6 amaretti cookies, crushed (about ¼ cup)

¾ pound fresh whole-milk ricotta cheese (1½ cups)

½ cup sugar

½ cup almond flour

⅝ teaspoon salt

1 teaspoon vanilla extract

Zest of 1 orange

5 large egg whites, at room temperature

Preheat the oven to 350°F, placing a rack in the lower third. Grease a 2-quart soufflé dish. Line the prepared dish evenly with the amaretti crumbs.

Stir together the ricotta, sugar, almond flour, salt, vanilla, and orange zest in a medium bowl.

In a stand mixer fitted with the whisk, beat the egg whites on medium-high speed until they're firm and form stiff peaks. Using a rubber spatula, gently fold the ricotta mixture into the egg whites, one-third at a time, in a figure-eight shape, while simultaneously spinning the bowl to guide you.

Pour the mixure into the soufflé dish and gently even out the top with a spatula. Bake until the top is set and the edges are beginning to turn golden, or until a cake tester inserted in the center comes out clean, about 40 minutes.

Serve immediately. Leftover soufflé can be stored in an airtight container in the refrigerator overnight and is quite good cold.

APPENDIX A: DISHES BY COURSE

APPETIZERS

Cauliflower à la Prune
(The Restaurant)
Cornmeal-Crusted Calamari
with Red Pepper Chutney
Crab Salad Hand Rolls
Curry-Roasted Carrots with
Cashew-Coconut Cream
Flatbread with Potatoes,
Mushrooms & Taleggio
Minty-Fresh Zucchini Salad
with Marinated Feta
Onion Risotto
Pappa al Pomodoro
Radicchio, Prune & Pork Belly
Salad
Ricotta & Tomatoes
on Toast
Salmon Tartare with Peas
& Pickled Celery Root
Savory Apple Tarte Tatin
Slow-Cooked Zucchini with
Ground Pistachios
Spaghetti with Crab, Lemon
& Nori
Strawberry Tomato Salad

BREAKFAST/BRUNCH

Apple-Oat Scones
Congee with All the Fixings
Crab Salad Hand Rolls
Crunchy Coconut Rice
Egg Salad
Fool's Ful
Grilled Chocolate
Sandwiches
Labneh-Baked Eggs
Onion Tart
Potato Hash
Recooked Beans

Rice Omelet
Shrimp & Tomato Salad
Slow-Scrambled Eggs with
Olive Tapenade
Smoky Strata

CONDIMENTS

Amaretti Crunch
Buttermilk Dressing
Cashew-Coconut Cream
Cashew Sauce
Chili Oil
Chili Powder
Chocolate Sauce
Eggplant Smour
Hummus
Lime Vinaigrette
Miso-Mustard Dressing
Olive Oil–Custard Sauce
Olive Tapenade
Orange Curd
Parsnip Relish
Pesto
Pickled Celery Root
Pickled Prunes
Pine Nut Butter
Red Pepper Chutney
Savory Granola
Spiced Cashews
Tahini Crema
Tartar Sauce

DESSERTS

Carrot Upside-Down Cake
Chocolate Bread Pudding
Grilled Chocolate Sandwiches
Orange-Ricotta Soufflé
Ricotta Gelato Coppetta
Semifreddo Tartine with
Chocolate Sauce

Strawberries with Whipped
Goat Cheese & Balsamic
Syrup
Strawberry Shortcake
Sweet Potato Pie
Zucchini Bread

HORS D'OEUVRES

Crab Salad Hand Rolls
Flatbread with Potatoes,
Mushrooms & Taleggio
Rice Fritters
Ricotta & Tomatoes on Toast
Salmon Tartare with Peas &
Pickled Celery Root
Slow-Cooked Zucchini with
Ground Pistachios

MAIN COURSES/MEALS

Braised Pork Belly with Prunes
& Radicchio
Broccoli Braised in Olive Oil
Cauliflower à la Prune (The
Restaurant)
Cauliflower Gratin
A Chicken in Every Pot
Chicken Paillard & Arugula
Salad with Marinated
Mozzarella
Chicken Salad Goma-ae
Christine's Chicken with
Roasted Apples & Shallots
Congee with All the Fixings
Crab Cakes with Tartar Sauce
Crab Salad Hand Rolls
Creamed Leeks with Roasted
Broccoli
Crunchy Coconut Rice
Curry-Roasted Carrots with
Cashew-Coconut Cream

Eggplant-Beef Burgers with
 Parsnip Relish
Egg Salad
Flatbread with Potatoes,
 Mushrooms & Taleggio
Fool's Ful
Hoecake with Stir-Fried Squid
 & Peppers
Kerala-Style Lamb Stew
Labneh-Baked Eggs
Lamb, Date & Chickpea
 Pilaf
Minty-Fresh Zucchini Salad
 with Marinated Feta
NYC Shepherd's Moussaka
Oatotto with Apples
One-Pan Peas 'n' Salmon
Onion Risotto
Onion Tart
Pappa al Pomodoro
Parsnippy Bobotie with
 Eggplant Smoor
Potato-Chip Crusted Chicken
 with Arugula Pesto
A Pot of Beans
Radicchio, Prune & Pork Belly
 Salad
Rice Omelet
Roasted Lamb Pitas with
 Hummus
Roasted Salmon with Cast-Iron
 Celery Root & Green Pea
 Mash
Sauced Roasted Cauliflower
Saucy Peppers, Polenta &
 Boiled Squid
Savory Apple Tarte Tatin
Shrimp & Tomato Salad
Slow-Cooked Zucchini with
 Ground Pistachios

Smoky Strata
Stir-Fried Pork Belly with
 Pickled Prunes

PASTAS

Actually Good Noodle Casserole
Oatotto with Apples
Onion Risotto
Orecchiette with Broccoli Rabe
Pasta Salad with Miso-Mustard
 Dressing
Pasta with Sicilian-Style Pesto
 & Shrimp
Spaghetti with Crab, Lemon &
 Nori
Whole-Wheat Pasta with
 Amaretti, Orange & Ricotta

SALADS

Apple Salad with Savory
 Granola
Arugula Salad with Marinated
 Mozzarella
Chicken Salad Goma-ae
Egg Salad
Minty-Fresh Zucchini Salad
 with Marinated Feta
New Potato Salad
Pasta Salad with Miso-Mustard
 Dressing
Radicchio, Prune & Pork Belly
 Salad
Shrimp & Tomato Salad
Strawberry Tomato Salad
Thai-ish Carrot Salad

SIDES

Baked Sweet Potatoes with
 Tahini Crema
Broccoli Braised in Olive Oil

Cauliflower à la Prune
 (The Restaurant)
Chickpeas
Creamed Leeks with Roasted
 Broccoli
Curry-Roasted Carrots with
 Cashew-Coconut Cream
Eggplant Smoor
New Potato Salad
A Pot of Beans
Recooked Beans
Rice Fritters
Roasted Apples & Shallots
Sauced Roasted Cauliflower
Slow-Cooked Zucchini with
 Ground Pistachios
Sweet Potato Casserole with
 Tahini Fluff

SNACKS

Apple-Oat Scones
Carrot Upside-Down Cake
Grilled Chocolate Sandwiches
Rice Fritters
Zucchini Bread

SOUPS

Almond Soup with Shrimp &
 Candied Tomatoes
Broccoli Leek Soup
Fool's Ful

APPENDIX B: RESOURCES

As a food writer, I've spent a lot of time seeking and testing products. Here are some of the brands and stores I go back to and recommend.

Anson Mills / ansonmills.com
Carolina Gold rice, cornmeal, grits, polenta

Artisana Organics / artisanaorganics.com
Coconut oil

BLiS / blisgourmet.com
Maple syrup

Bob's Red Mill / bobsredmill.com
Almond flour, coconut sugar, oats

Brightland/brightland.co
Extra-virgin olive oil

Carr's Ciderhouse / carrsciderhouse.com
Cider vinegar

Daphnis and Chloe / daphnisandchloe.com
Dried herbs, smoked dried red chili flakes

Georgia Grinders / georgiagrinders.com
Almond butter, cashew butter

The Japanese Pantry / thejapanesepantry.com
Rice vinegar, sesame oil, soy sauce

June Taylor Jams / junetaylorjams.com
Jam

La Tienda /tienda.com
Sherry vinegar, olive oil–conserved seafood

Maille / maille.com
Dijon mustard, honey mustard

The Meadow / themeadow.com
Salt

New York Shuk / nyshuk.com
Harissa

Rancho Gordo / ranchogordo.com
Marcella beans (i.e., Italian Sorana cannellinis)

See Smell Taste / seesmelltaste.com
Pimentón de la Vera and other spices

Koda Farms / kodafarms.com
Kokuho Rose medium-grain rice

Snuk/snukfoods.com
Date syrup, pomegranate molasses, spices

Sonoma Syrup Co. / sonomasyrup.com
Vanilla Bean Extract "Crush"

Soom / soomfoods.com
Tahini

Valrhona / valrhona-chocolate.com
Baking chocolate, cocoa powder

Whole Foods / wholefoodsmarket.com
Labneh (if not available in a local gourmet shop)

ACKNOWLEDGMENTS

Thank you to my friends and family who listened to me moan and groan about everything, every step of the way; who ate the food shoved in their faces; and who took the leftovers foisted on them.

One of the best and most motivating parts of working on this cookbook was being reunited with Aubrie Pick (and Bessma Khalaf) and Stephanie Huntwork. Aubrie shot my first cookbook and I insisted or begged (depending on whom you ask) that she shoot this one too—not just because she's so talented, quick-thinking, creative, and scarily efficient, but also because she's an awesome, true-blue human being. *And look at the photographs! My god!* Aubrie, you're the reason this cookbook is something to behold . . . well, you, and Stephanie!

Stephanie, can we just have regular meetings at Kitchen Arts & Letters to talk about whatever we feel like and flip through cookbooks while we peruse? Thank you for your intuition, vision, and taste. And for bringing your good energy to every situation.

Bessma, sometimes, when it feels like the walls are caving in, I go back to that video of you doing your martial arts exercise and chopping at the air. I don't ever want to be on a set without you!

Special thanks, too, to Lillian Kang—aka Mrs. Mochi—for the happy place in Berkeley, and for showing me what an exemplary food stylist looks like and how to get the job done. You and Veronica Laramie were—and are—incredible. (Veronica, every time I see caramelized sweet potato goo, I think of you!) Alexis Mersel, we had only a day to get to know each other, but your contributions (biscuit making included) were vital and it was a pleasure meeting you. Props to Ethel Brennan, especially for the Heller pieces.

Although you've traded in measuring cups for decanters and are now heavy into the world of wine, and on your way to one day becoming a master sommelier, should you ever get tired of all that tilting and swirling and sniffing and sipping, you should know, you're one hell of a recipe tester, Lily Freedman.

Laura Nolan, if I just say "thanks" would that seem like a throwaway? Probably. But at this point, after all these years and projects, I can't find the right words. Maybe "thank you for putting up with me"? Is that better? Or, I know, "thank you for having my back and continuing to push whenever I declare I've given up."

To the team at Clarkson Potter: Cookbooks are collaborative. I definitely could not have done this without you. Some of you were more directly involved and had more visible, substantial roles in the process (hi, Amanda E. and Gabbie V.T., and, in the early days, Angelin B.); but I know there are many of you behind the scenes doing work quietly. I want to thank *all* of you.

Pawstein, kisses.

INDEX

Note: Page references in *italics* indicate photographs.

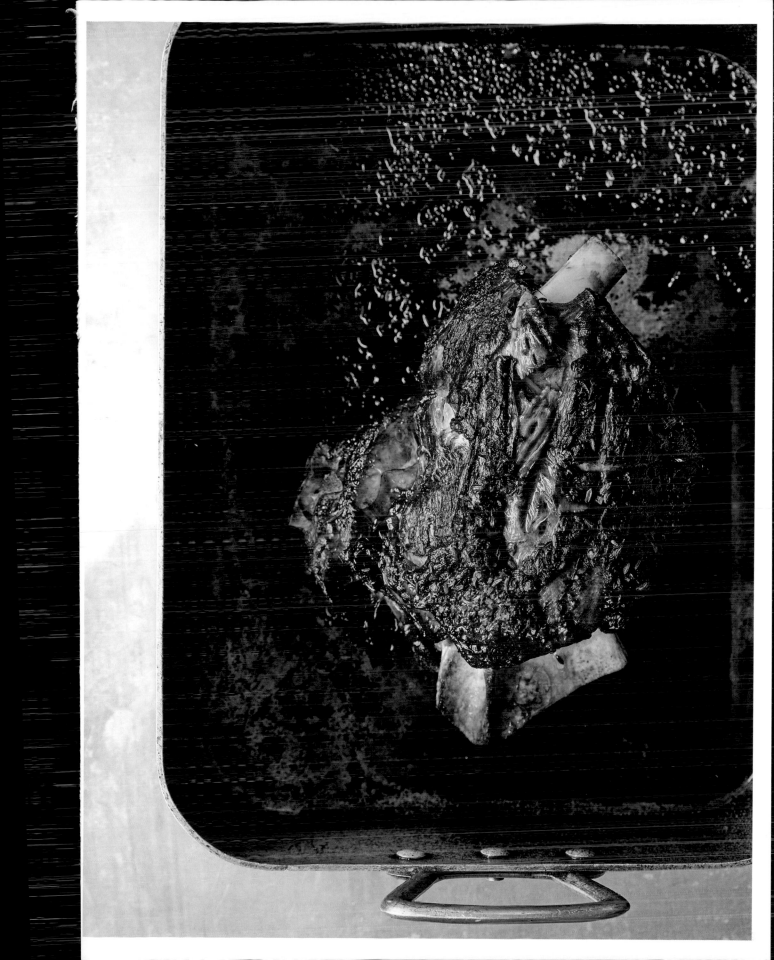